CW01095954

Around The World I

The Amazing Story Of The Islington Corinthians
1937/38 World Tour

Rob Cavallini

British Library Cataloguing in Publication Data
A catalogue record for this book is available from the British Library
ISBN 978-0-9550496-1-3

Published by Dog N Duck Publications

Printed and bound in Great Britain by 4edge Ltd, Hockley. www.4edge.co.uk

Cover design by Mick Magic

Contents

INTRODUCTION

I first stumbled across the Islington Corinthians world tour of 1937/38 by accident whilst researching the Corinthian F.C. As I continued researching, my eyes were constantly being attracted to the exotic locations and the sheer scale of the tour which they undertook in the days before international travel was commonplace. Calcutta, Singapore, Manila, Japan and Honolulu all cropped up and I could only marvel at what an experience this must have been for the players. This was even more remarkable when put in context with the prevailing world events, which were to culminate a year after their return in the form of World War Two.

My interest was reawoken a year or so later when Sian Murphy the grand-daughter of A.J. Martin, contacted me in regard to the Corinthian FC and inquired whether this was the same club as the Islington Corinthians. It is not, of course, but I resolved on being shown the scrapbooks Sian's grandfather (A.J. Martin) had kept, that this story (which has almost been airbrushed from history) should be told.

Why are the Islington Corinthians forgotten? This is conjecture, as maybe the story was just 'lost' in the Second World War, but it may have been deliberately ignored by the post-war amateur football writers (who were largely ex-Corinthian) because the club had the impertinence to use such a famous name in their title. It was (and remains) by far the biggest tour ever undertaken by a British team, but next to nothing has been written about the club. The exceptions are Bob Alaway's book *'Football All Around the World*,' and a handful of mentions during the tour in *The Times* and other national newspapers. Surprisingly the world wide web throws up only a few references, usually with regard to development of football in India, Pakistan and Japan.

Fortunately from the research point of view, the I.C.'s played in countries with strong British connections and consequently English language newspapers. Colindale Newspaper Library has collected these over the years and I discovered an abundance of material which I had not really anticipated finding. The Islington Corinthians were, as I was to discover, a huge attraction in most places that they visited and many column inches were devoted to the club's exploits and their genial secretary Tom Smith, who was always willing to tell a story.

In this book I have attempted to construct an accurate record of the club's short existence, whilst focusing on the mother of all tours. Tom Smith and Pat Clark's memories feature strongly as they were the two dominant characters who recorded their experiences. Without their contributions in the press and Alaway's book, this story could not have been told.

Touring was not a new invention in 1937, the first UK based tours having been undertaken by the Wanderers F.C. in the 1860's, whilst the first overseas tour dates back to 1890 when Clapton F.C. visited Antwerp and defeated a Belgium XI 8-1. This started a trend and was taken up by many of the amateur and professional clubs. The Corinthian F.C. and Civil Service were the leading lights in this area, with the former going further afield than any other club visiting America, Brazil, Canada and South Africa before World War One. The Civil Service famously recorded the scalps of Real Madrid, Barcelona, Atletico Bilbao and Slavia Prague amongst others.

The most common time for tours in the early days was at Easter and it was not uncommon to see the majority of the leading amateur clubs departing to the continent for a week and taking on the leading clubs from the country they were visiting.

From this humble beginning the football tour has continued, with Middlesex Wanderers, for example, still visiting distant and exotic places. Today, however, the big clubs only seem use it as an excuse to pick up easy money in the Far-East or America, whilst clubs such as the team I support, Grimsby Town, have ended up playing in tournaments in Ibiza, that well-known footballing hotbed, against the local sides. All this aside, a football tour is one of the most positive contributions to friendship between countries that can be made, and the good-will that is generated from these visits lasts for many years.

As a veteran of five football tours, three (USA, Brazil and China) as an official and two as a supporter, I have made many friends and enjoyed experiences beyond my wildest dreams. I can only imagine in wonderment what the Islington Corinthians' players and officials might have been thinking about during their world tour. They could have had little idea of what they would see or witness, in these days before mass television audiences, and images in the cinema from distant countries were few. Perhaps the more well-read members of the party may have spent the months leading up to the trip studying travel books, but I am sure that these could not have prepared them for the events and sights which were awaiting them as the tour progressed into the unknown.

Rob Cavallini
2008

CHAPTER ONE

THE EARLY DAYS 1932-1936

The Islington Corinthians began life on Monday 6th June 1932 at a meeting commissioned by the enigmatic Tom Smith. Smith's original blueprint for the club sought only to provide interesting games for the early closing day in Islington and to assist deserving charities, but it was to exceed by far these humble intentions and in Smith they had a leader whose showman tendencies were never far from the surface. With Smith being the dynamic force behind the new club, it is perhaps safe to assume that it was he who came up with the name Islington Corinthians. Clearly this was inspired by the famous Corinthian F.C. who had travelled the globe, and also taken on leading professional clubs and beaten them. Arranging foreign tours may have been Smith's intention from the start as he was certainly well travelled, and was to lead a delegation from the Islington Rotary Club on a trip to Yugoslavia in May 1934.

Smith addressed the first meeting with the following words:

'Explaining his proposition, Councillor Tom Smith said that his travels round football grounds on Saturday afternoons had brought him in contact with a number of well known amateur players who were willing to play on Thursday afternoons. The idea was to have two, or possibly three, teams, the first eleven, which would include high class amateur players, to play at Tufnell Park. Although time was getting short, Councillor Smith thought it would be possible to arrange an attractive fixture list for next season. The Northern Polytechnic had kindly consented to allow the use of the Tufnell Park ground on very favourable terms. The second and third elevens were designed to attract young Islington footballers, and Councillor Smith explained that Mr. W. Jelks, Past President of the Islington Rotary Club, had put in his way a field allowing room for a full size football pitch, at the back of 'The Grange,' Whetstone. The reserve teams could be entered for cup contests. With these facilities in hand, he believed they could have a really good Islington Club and they wanted the public of Islington to back up the local leaders and businessmen who were taking an interest in the project.'[1]

It was also agreed that the club would affiliate to the London Football Association and that the club would be known as the Islington Corinthians, unless this proved unacceptable to their parent body and then it would simply be known as Islington F.C. The colours were decided as being white shirts with dark blue facings and cuffs and membership was set at one guinea. Alderman Sargent presented the first ball to the club, whilst Tom Smith undertook the responsibility for the first year's rent at the ground in Whetstone. A second meeting was held on 19th July at Northern Polytechnic to adopt rules, elect officers and register players, when nearly 40 players signed up for the club.

The founder, Tom Smith who lived in Harrow, was a Chartered Masseur and Electrotherapeutist by profession, also a local councillor (1931-1934), a prominent local business man and Rotarian who was an immense football enthusiast. His active interest in the sport began in 1902 when he jointly founded the Old Hanoverians for former pupils of the Hanover Street Elementary School, which was close to the canal basins of the Grand Union Canal. Their first team by the time the Islington Corinthians had been founded were playing in the Northern Suburban Intermediate League.

In the early 1920's, Smith joined the Tufnell Park Football Club, a name now almost forgotten to all but the most studious of football historians. Tufnell Park were in fact a big name in amateur football between the two world wars and competed in London's premier amateur football competition, the Isthmian League, during this period. They still exist today, but several name changes and mergers later came to their present name, Haringey Borough. Tufnell Park's greatest achievement, however, came just prior to Smith's arrival when they were runners-up in the 1920 F.A. Amateur Cup final. Smith eventually became Chairman of Tufnell Park F.C. between the years of 1929 and 1932, when he relinquished the post and founded the Islington Corinthians.

Tufnell Park F.C. played at the Recreation Ground, in Campdale Road, although it has been given a variety of names since The Casuals first moved there in 1896. Those names include Junction Road, which lies close to the London underground station, Huddleston Road and sometimes the Tufnell Park Athletic Ground. It once boasted an impressive grandstand, and was regularly used for athletics and cricket. It still exists today with its distinct football ground shape, but any remnants of the stadium have long since gone. The stadium's proudest moment was perhaps hosting the F.A. Amateur Cup final in 1897, and it was here that the Islington Corinthians would call home.

During Smith's tenure as Tufnell Park Chairman, there was a split within the club and the whole first team left. He solved this crisis by obtaining the entire Leyton team, who were available after the Essex F.A. had suspended that club. Smith's other football interests included being involved in the Highbury Traders, who became Highbury Thursdays (an indication of where his affection for mid week football arose).

Smith was continually on the lookout for new ideas and challenges and later reminisced about the formation of the Islington Corinthians:

'We realised that we had got here in North London the finest professional side in England, and we thought at the same time we should like to have in Islington the best amateur side.'

At first they were told that the idea for forming a strong Thursday Club had been attempted several times, but had never been a success, and that this venture could not possibly last a year. 'We did last a year!' said Mr. Smith 'and we very soon found that, far from being against the idea, professional clubs were really very friendly and helpful.'[2]

The borough of Islington offered the club the chance to succeed and it was now London's second largest borough (behind Wandsworth) with a population of 327,403 in 1931. From the outset the Islington Corinthians had strong backers, including the Islington Rotary Club, and largely due to Smith's contacts could boast of having the Marquess of Northampton D.S.O. as president, and the Mayor of Islington, Miss Thelma Cazalet L.C.C. (later to become a governor of the B.B.C. between 1957-1962), M.P., Mr T.F. Howard M.P., Mr. Patrick Donner M.P., Colonel A.W. Goodman M.P. (the four M.P.'s for Islington), and Lieut.-Commander R.L. Tufnell M.P., and Mr J. Oudheusen (of Ajax) as vice-presidents. The other committee members were equally impressive with Alderman F. Leydon Sargent (who was knighted in 1939) taking the role of Chairman, Tom Smith as Secretary and Mr. Charles R. Andrew of the Westminster Bank as Treasurer. This roll-call of local grandees probably explains why the club was allowed to use the Islington Coat of Arms as its emblem, whilst Smith's football connections secured the use of the Tufnell Park enclosure for home games.

1932/33

The fledgling Islington Corinthian club, with Arsenal's Tom Parker as coach, began their inaugural season with an interesting programme of friendly fixtures, whilst fielding an 'A' team in the North London Thursday League and a 'B' team in the Hendon League.

On the 8th September 1932, the new club faced Barnet Thursday (the reigning North London Thursday League champions) at Tufnell Park. The ground had been decorated with flags and bunting to mark the occasion through the kindness of T.R. Roberts, and Sir Frederick Wall, Chairman of the Football Association was in attendance. Bad weather, however, dissuaded the Islington public from attending in great numbers, but when E.Hankin led his men from the dressing room, they were given cordial cheers by those in the crowd.

ISLINGTON CORINTHIANS 1 BARNET THURSDAY 1

'The Corinthians had the advantage of the slope and early in the proceedings Lockey tested Gilroy. The Okin-Cowan wing was prominent with a pretty run. Okin fired over from six yards.

W. Lockey struck the cross-bar with a great drive after a combined run on the Corinthians left wing. A minute later the same player fired just over.

The Corinthians were overplaying their opponents at this juncture, only weak finishing preventing a score.

Gaunt forced a corner and later Wade headed out one of Lockey's expresses as it was entering the net.

Gilroy saved finely from Okin, and for half an hour the play greatly favoured the new club.

After a time Barnet had a fair share of the game, but during a Corinthian raid Okin again was too lofty with his shooting.

BARNET SCORE FIRST
Greatly against the run of the game, Barnet took the lead. Keizer caught a centre from Parker, but before he could clear Winchester charged him over the line with the ball in his possession.

Resuming Barnet had more of the game but Hankins and Downs defended with determination and skill. Wade at left back for Barnet was a difficult man to beat. Gilroy saved finely from Lockey and a minute later repeated the feat.

Within 30 seconds Lockey hit an upright and Cowan was wide from six yards and Lockey fired over from a rebound.

The Barnet goal bore a charmed life and nothing went right for the Corinthians.

Following a combined movement up the middle Gaunt equalised for the Corinthians. Gilroy having no chance.'[3]

The first team continued strongly and by Christmas 1932 had lost just one game (narrowly by the odd goal in three) to the professional side, Clapton Orient. The high point was a 1-0 win over a Crystal Palace XI and a 2-1 victory over Isthmian League club, London Caledonians. Success had been achieved against a couple of less than illustrious names such as the South East London Thursday League and Clapton Thursday. A game against Arsenal had to be postponed due to Tufnell Park needing the ground for a cup replay. The local press had also warmed to the club and from November they were given a weekly front page column in the Islington Gazette.

The club was building a fine reputation for itself and 500 people attended an 'A' team game against Manor Park Thursday, an impressive figure for a non first team game. The first team not to be outdone collected its first piece of silverware in January when, in a game ruined by fog, Covent Garden were defeated 3-2 in the St. Peter's Hospital Cup at Wimbledon. Smith arranged for players and supporters to be transported to the game by charabancs with match tickets combined with a return ticket priced at three shillings and sixpence.

Smith's idea was beginning to bear fruit and clearly his self belief was justified as the Islington Corinthians recorded their finest result to date in February.

ISLINGTON CORINTHIANS 3 CLAPTON ORIENT 2

'The first team continued their run of success last week by a brilliant victory over Clapton Orient by three goals to two. Forced through illness and other causes to field a weak side, they were quickly in arrears, and twenty minutes after the start went further behind from a penalty kick awarded against Gilbey. Before the interval, however, Hankins, who was playing centre forward, reduced the lead, and the interval score was 1-2.

The second half provided a memorable display. The Corinthians pressed continually, and only magnificent play by the Orient backs kept the home side from scoring, shots by Marrable, Cowan and Hankins being headed out from under the bar, with the goal keeper beaten. Two splendid goals by Hankins sealed the issue, and we ran out winners of a fast and exciting game by three goals to two.'[4]

The club's first social function was also held around the time of this match when a Great Whist Drive was held at the Town Hall. The I.C.'s, as they were often known in the press, were clearly a very sociable and hospitable club. Following a 3-1 victory over the Grenadier Guards at Tufnell Park both teams dined at the Tufnell Park Hotel then proceeded to a dance at Stanley Hall. The following letter from the visitors appeared in the Islington Gazette shortly afterwards:

'Dear Mr. Smith, - On behalf of the Football Club I would like to express both to you and the members of your club our deepest thanks for the wonderful time you gave us on Thursday last. I know full well that all of us appreciate it very much and we only hope that we may in some way be able to repay you at some later date. Again thanking you for your kindness.'[5]

Tom Smith's next idea smacked of genius and really helped create a firm foundation for the club to build on. Smith, capitalising on the shockwaves created by the humbling of the mighty Arsenal by lowly Walsall in the F.A. Cup in January, invited the famous giant killers to visit Tufnell Park. The I.C.'s were hoping to attract a record attendance to Tufnell Park, and readily paid a guarantee of £100 to the professionals. Smith's coup in attracting the Midland side created a buzz around the town, and one

11

month prior to the game all the two shilling seats had sold out and only a few three and five shilling seats were available. Standing tickets were available on the day at seven pence and it was hoped that a capacity crowd of 6,000 would be recorded. Smith even employed sandwich-board men to advertise the game outside Highbury Stadium in the weeks leading up to the match.

The Islington Corinthians were aiming to put on a show and the following amateurs, G.P. Keizer (Q.P.R.), Jack Burns (Brentford and London Caledonians) and F. Okin (Kingstonian) all accepted invitations to guest for the team. Unfortunately A.H. Fabian, the famous Corinthian, could not appear as he was due to play for Derby County in the forthcoming F.A. Cup semi-final.

Of those mentioned, Gerrit Keizer was a particularly interesting character. He was a goal-keeper and one of Arsenal's earliest Dutch imports, when Herbert Chapman signed him from Margate (which became Arsenal's nursery team in 1934) and immediately selected him for the first team. Keizer collected a F.A. Charity Shield winner's medal and appeared in the first twelve matches of the 1930/31 season. Whilst playing for Arsenal he earned the nickname 'The Flying Dutchman' as he would travel back to Amsterdam to play for Ajax's reserves on a Sunday! It is reported that he had a distinctly flamboyant, if erratic style and this is what cost him his place in the Arsenal side. He later moved to Charlton and then on to Q.P.R., before settling back home in Amsterdam in 1933, playing out the rest of his career with Ajax. He appeared in a World Cup qualifying match for Holland against Belgium which ensured their qualification for the 1934 finals, although he failed to make the squad for the championships in Italy. Later in life he travelled to London and persuaded Arsenal to donate a set of kit and footballs for Ajax who were struggling financially after the war. Keizer continued to make trips across the Channel, and in 1947 was arrested for smuggling British bank notes amongst the sportswear and was sentenced to six months imprisonment.

The I.C.'s and the Islington Rotary Club entertained their famous visitors to lunch at Beale's Resturant, where the Mayor of Islington made a welcoming address. There was an illustrious company in attendance as Sir Frederick Wall, and the referee for the game, (the future Sir) Stanley Rous were both present, as well as the managers of Q.P.R., Fulham and Southampton, Archie Mitchell, Jimmy McIntyre and George Kay respectively.

The two clubs certainly appreciated the spirit of the occasion and the professionals fielded all but one of their team that defeated Arsenal, whilst the Islington Corinthians fielded a team containing an amateur international in the form of Ling, plus Hankins, Vierant and Downs of Tufnell Park, and Couchman (a last minute replacement for Burns), Okin and Keizer as previously mentioned. Despite two high-class teams being on display and the early promising ticket sales, a steady drizzle on the day of the match affected the game and a substantial loss was incurred. Smith, after the game suggested that the Islington Rotary Club were the financial losers when he said: '*Without the*

12

*Rotary Club we could not have gone through with the match.'*₆ Two people who did attend were the Arsenal stars Joe Hulme and David Jack who were to see the only side from Islington to score against Walsall that year!

ISLINGTON CORINTHIANS 1 WALSALL 3

'Corinthians began with the slope in their favour, but Walsall were the first to become dangerous, Keizer being fully tested in saving a hot shot from Ball at expense of a corner. The opening exchanges were keenly contested, the amateurs fully holding their own. Keizer next merely fielded a ball from Alsop, who later was penalised for fouling the goal keeper. Saggers burst through at the other end, but was crowded out. A long shot by Cox was easily saved.

Considering the climate conditions the quality of the football was quite good. The professionals were much smarter on the ball, but tenacious defence kept the Walsall attack in check for twenty minutes. A good piece of work by Viereant was applauded. Keizer continued in good form, his 'hands' being very safe, some of his work being loudly applauded. Hankins nipped in when Alsop was almost through, and later Saggers was offside with an open goal gapping in front of him.

Walsall had a fine opportunity of opening their account, but three men in succession missed. A long shot by Cox – from a free kick – was punched clear by Cunningham, and for a time Corinthians were dangerous, a shot by Couchman going a foot wide. Walsall were very fortunate in opening their account, a shot by Shepherd finding its way into the net helped by Ling. A good movement by the Corinthian left wing was nipped in the bud through offside. Lee proved too good for the opposing defence and working an opening for Shepherd, the latter added a second for Walsall, the ball going into the net off the far post. Saggers narrowly missed with a good shot that was only inches wide. A splendid movement on the Corinthians' right saw Gilderson's final shot crowded out. At half-time, Walsall led 2-0.

Just after resuming Keizer made a magnificent save from Lee and later distinguished himself again from the same player. Shepherd completed his hat trick with a beautiful oblique shot that gaze Keizer no chance. A lovely first-timer by Alsop was magnificently saved by the Corinthians keeper. The home defence were now having a lively time, although from a breakaway things looked dangerous. Keizer went down very pluckily to Alsop's feet, thereby saving a certain goal.

*Towards the close the Corinthians showed signs of distress, and Walsall were right on top, relieved only by an occasional raid by the home wingers. Okin aroused the enthusiasm of the spectators by carefully lobbing the ball over the backs' heads to score a clever goal when Cunningham was out of position. Corinthians may thus claim to have accomplished a feat the Arsenal did not.'*₇

Islington Corinthians bounced back from this defeat by winning the Woolfe Cup in aid of the Royal Northern Hospital, overcoming the previously unbeaten Market Bridge 4-3 and raising £50 for charity in the process. Another impressive result was recorded with a 1-1 draw against Charlton Athletic which was described as 'the best exhibition so far given at the park,' but the first bad run in the club's history then followed. A 0-4 defeat against Leytonstone (who only lost the Isthmian League championship on goal average that season) was then followed by a 4-5 defeat at Athenian League Redhill when the side rallied from 0-5 down to give the scoreline an air of respectability. The last reported game of the season was against Tottenham Hotspur and another poor attendance witnessed a commendable 1-1 draw with newly appointed Islington Corinthian player-manager, Sid Marrable, putting his team in front.

The first season certainly got the new club off to a fine start and their honours along with the two previous mentioned successes included the St.Peter's Hospital Cup, and the Hungerford six-a-side Cup (I.C.'s were the first London club to win this for 40 years.), The 'B' team lifted the Hendon Thursday League Challenge Cup, whilst the 'A' team won the North London Thursday League.

In the close season, a reorganisation was announced with the club being split into Senior and Junior sections and Dave Clark of Highbury F.C. being appointed secretary of the Juniors.

North London Thursday League Division One 1932/33					
	P	W	D	L	Pts
Islington Corinthians	18	15	0	3	30
Tottenham Police	18	12	3	3	27
North London B.T.	18	11	1	6	23
The Fox	18	9	1	8	19
Barnet Thursday	18	9	0	9	18
Belmont 'A'	18	6	5	7	17
Walthamstow Argyle	18	6	4	8	16
Metropolitan Electric Trams	18	4	4	10	12
Clapton Thursday 'A'	18	3	4	11	10
The Grange	18	3	2	13	8

1933/34

The second season of the Islington Corinthians promised even more excitement for the club members as, following on from their fine performance the previous season, the club was accepted into the London Professional Midweek League and plans for their first visit overseas were unveiled. The London Professional Midweek League was played for during the 1930's, as a way of giving clubs extra games. It was a small league which consisted of a mixture of professional clubs' reserves and 'A' sides with a couple of amateur teams at varying times. Smith was working hard at further establishing the club as a football force and knew how to engage the media:

'In a chat with their wonderful and enthusiastic Hon. Secretary, Tom Smith, whose vitality is so contagious I find that Islington Corinthians are making real and substantial progress. Numerous applications have been received for membership and some weeks as many as five matches will be played – two in mid-week and three on Saturdays. Patrons and supporters will have an opportunity of witnessing football by the following famous clubs, who are due to play at Tufnell Park: Arsenal, Brentford, Guildford, Charlton, West Ham, Clapton Orient, Ramsgate, Dartford, Grenadier Guards, Chelsea, Park Royal, Gillingham, etc. '[8]

Prior to this the club had made an announcement about a tour to Holland, one suspects through Smith's dealings with Keizer:

'An attractive opening will be provided by a tour to Holland, which will be made at the invitation of the Dutch Football Association, from August 20th to 30th. Five matches will be played and the Corinthians' opponents will include well-known Netherlands's football teams.

In the coming season the Corinthians will compete in the London Professional Mid-week League, which will bring them into rivalry with the leading London Clubs. Their opening match will be at Tufnell Park on September 7th, when Charlton Athletic will be the visitors'[9]

This initial tour became an on-off affair as their Dutch hosts wanted to move the dates of the visit, which led to an announcement that it had been cancelled in late August as all the players had already arranged their holiday dates and could not change them at short notice. In the space of two weeks, however, a satisfactory compromise was reached and the Islington Gazette announced that the tour was back on, but only for two games, which later became one.

The Islington Corinthians warmed up for their visit to Amsterdam when a weak team lost 0-3 at home to Charlton Athletic in early September. The visit to Amsterdam was not widely reported and only a brief account has been traced, no details being known about the trip other than this:

AJAX 4 ISLINGTON CORINTHIANS 0

'On Sunday, at Amsterdam, before a crowd numbering 10,000, they met the Ajax Club, a Dutch senior team and were defeated by four goals to nil. The play was by no means one-sided. In mid-field there was little to chose between the team, but the Ajax forwards were the better marksmen. Their centre forward scored three fine goals. The Corinthians thoroughly enjoyed their visit to Holland and hope to have the opportunity of renewing acquaintances with the Ajax Club at Tufnell Park if the Dutch club's proposed visit to England matures.'[10]

On their return, Smith was busy using his Rotary connections for the benefit of the football club and had soon arranged a trip to Felixstowe. The event became a local who's who as the team was accompanied by the Mayor and Mayoress of Islington and a number of North London Rotarians. The coaches taking the party to Suffolk left Highbury station at 8.30 a.m. and arrived in time for lunch at the Grand Hotel, where they were welcomed by Mr.W.F. Cross, J.P. Chairman of Felixstowe Rotary Club and it is reported that: *'He wished the Corinthians the best of luck, but hoped that Felixstowe would win. (laughter)'*11 The hospitality was extended further by their hosts and the afternoon was spent at the Summer Theatre in Ranelagh Gardens, where a special performance was given by Rotarian Wilby Lunn's Concert Party. There was still time to fit in a football match and the I.C.'s recorded a comfortable 4-0 victory over their hosts. Late in the game Islington were awarded a penalty, but honouring the name Corinthian, A.E. Hankin made no effort to score as they felt it was accidental.

The following week another Rotary event was organised at Walsall where the two clubs from the previous season's encounter were to meet again. It was another strong Rotarian contingent who went in support, some fourteen in all, and they were accompanied by Tom Howard D.C.M., L.C.C., M.P., Jimmy McIntyre of Fulham and Mr. J. Oudheusen the treasurer of Ajax. The football match again ended in favour of Walsall although the I.C.'s performed well losing only 3-5 after leading 2-1 at half time. As a result of this game, indeed immediately after the match, McIntyre signed the Islington goal-keeper Savio as an amateur for Fulham.

On the 12th October 1933, Islington Corinthians made their debut in the London Professional Midweek League, by facing Guildford City at Tufnell Park. The amateurs went in a goal down at the interval, but two goals by Tomlinson in the space of three second half minutes got the club's new venture off to a successful start.

Another of Tom Smith's forward thinking ideas came to fruition in the week following this game, when the club's new social club was opened at 277 City Road by Alderman F. Leydon Sargent. If nothing else this showed the ambition Smith had for his club and a detailed account is given here:

'The object of the Club is to provide a social meeting place for members and friends of the Islington Corinthians F.C. Excellent premises, which are to be known as the Café Corinth, are at the club's disposal. Several members of the Football Club have devoted much time of their leisure time of late to adapting the premises to the purposes of a social club. On the first floor is a hall that can be used for concerts, socials and the like, while in the basement a tea-lounge adjoins a billiard room, containing two full-size tables. A membership fee of 1s. per annum is charged, with an additional 2d. each time a member uses the Club. Both sexes are eligible for membership.

In introducing Alderman Sargent, Councillor Tom Smith, Hon. Secretary of the Club, said that they intended to keep their new venture as a temperance club and to form different sections to cater for the different interests of members. They had started, or would shortly start, sections for tennis, table-tennis, cricket, amateur theatrical's (including a concert party), and rambling; other sections would be initiated if not less than six members were interested. The Club would be opened on Sundays, when

16

competitions would be held among members, and he hoped to arrange dance classes. Councillor Smith added that they had already enrolled 80 members, and he hoped that by next week the number would reach 120. The premises could be extended if the need arose.

Alderman Sargent said that, as Chairman of Islington Corinthians' Football Club, he was pleased to open the Social Club and congratulate them on its institution. He thought it was a happy augury for the Club's future that its opening coincided with a splendid victory by the first team in their first match in the London Professional Mid-week League, and by the signal successes of the second and third teams in their matches. He was pleased to learn from Councillor Smith that several members had given their leisure time to fitting out the Club and with a continuation of that spirit, the success of their new venture was assured.

An excellent concert followed the opening ceremony.'[12]

Islington Corinthians, despite all their success achieved so far in a short space of time, could not maintain the momentum. The following week's friendly saw the club crash 4-10 to Charlton Athletic in an extraordinary game, where they did well to score four against strong opposition. West Ham United then inflicted their first league defeat on them, before Clapton Orient stormed to a 1-7 victory over the amateurs in a friendly match. After the game a supper and concert was held at the new social club, with tickets priced at two shillings and sixpence. The defeats continued to build up and Guildford City won the return league fixture 5-6 and then Dartford recorded an emphatic 0-4 victory before the close of 1933.

At the start of 1934 the Islington Corinthians were due to face one of their stiffest challenges so far, as the first fixture in January was against the mighty Arsenal. Arsenal included Dennis Compton in their side and they comfortably saw off the I.C.'s challenge 0-5, although the amateurs did improve when they had the advantage of the slope in the second half. Fortunately in their next league match the Islington Corinthians turned a corner in style by winning the return with Arsenal.

ISLINGTON CORINTHIANS 2 ARSENAL 1

'Considerable interest was taken in the professional mid-week match at Tufnell Park yesterday between the Islington Corinthians and Arsenal. Piquancy was added owing to the appearance of Joe Hulme, the celebrated international winger who had a try out following the removal of a cartilage. The conditions were favourable.

The Corinthians turned out a strong side and the Arsenal were well represented by promising juniors. Sir Samuel Hill Wood, Mr. George Allison and Mr. Joe Shaw were there and the game was supported by the Corinthians largest gate of the season.
For twenty minutes Arsenal did most of the pressing, but the Corinthians rallied and after Tomlinson had struck the cross-bar, the Corinthians centre forward scored twice in quick succession. Hankins playing at outside right, was largely responsible for the

17

first. The Tufs captain forced a corner and then beautifully placed the flag kick for Tomlinson to score. A pass up the middle enabled Tomlinson to flick the ball past the advancing Davies. At half-time the Corinthians were leading by two goals to nil.

The amateurs hardly deserved to lead by that margin, but they had certainly fully held their distinguished visitors. With the wind and slope in their favour the points looked good for the Corinthians and so it proved, for although Arsenal scored once through Carr, the balance of play was really with the Amateurs. Ted Hankins at outside right, did quite well and just before the close two stinging shots struck the crossbar within a minute. The Corinthians won by two goals to one and jolly well played.'[13]

Smith took advantage of such a positive result to try and get more local people involved in the club and launched the following appeal shortly after the game:

'The Islington Corinthians', who gained such a brilliant win over the Arsenal reserve side in the Mid-Week League, have passed through a very worrying period. To compete successfully with their professional rivals is a hard task at the best times, and during the last two months the calls of Saturday Cup-ties and representative games necessitated the turning out of depleted teams and the loss of points. Now that the club can call on its full strength, some very fine games should be seen during the rest of the season.

The public support at these games, however is essential, and a special appeal is made to the sportsmen of Islington to do their best to attend the remainder of the games and encourage others to do so. The club is trying hard to bring the best sides to Tufnell Park, and in return they have to travel long distances for return games. This year they have travelled to Walsall, Felixstowe, Ramsgate, Dartford, Guildford, Windsor and Tunbridge Wells, which has entailed considerable expense; and if these games are to be staged at Tufnell Park, good support is necessary.

Tradesmen who can show the weekly posters in prominent positions or put boards outside their shops can greatly assist, while there are vacancies for energetic sportsmen on the executive of the club for the various committees.

The club is the only amateur club in a professional league in England, and when playing its full strength can compete favourable with the very best sides. The club also encourages local talent, and as many as six teams have been put in the field during one week. These reserve sides are doing very well, being coached by old players, and before long it is hoped that Islington will have an amateur team to be proud of.'[14]

Islington Corinthians' good form continued as the 2nd Grenadier Guards were accounted for and then the St. Dunstan's Shield, in aid of blinded service men, was won after a 3-0 victory over the Post Office League. This game marked a milestone for the club's charitable donations as the club had now raised £200 for deserving causes. The last of a fine trio of victories passed almost without mention in the local

18

press, despite Chelsea being thrashed 4-0 at Tufnell Park in a league fixture. The run was ended in the next league game when champions elect Dartford won 1-2 to preserve their one hundred per cent league record.

Prior to the close of the season Islington Corinthians defeated Gillingham 3-2 away before losing 0-4 to Chelsea in the return league fixture at Stamford Bridge and 1-3 to Fulham at Tufnell Park.

London Professional Midweek League					
	P	W	D	L	Pts
Dartford	9	9	0	0	18
Chelsea	8	4	2	2	10
West Ham United	6	3	1	2	7
Guildford	7	3	0	4	6
Arsenal	8	3	0	5	6
Islington Corinthians	10	3	0	7	6
Park Royal	10	2	1	7	5

(Last available league table–up to 7.3.1934, but includes IC 0 Chelsea 4 and IC 1 Dartford 2)

The Islington Corinthians could take heart from a solid second season, with some creditable victories over the likes of Arsenal and Chelsea. The club was in a strong position and had won a considerable number of trophies including the St. Dunstan's Cup, Herbert Chapman Cup, and Royal Northern Hospital Cup (the latter as joint holders). They had retained the Hungerford six-a-side Cup and added to it the Woking six-a-side Cup in April. The lower teams had also performed admirably; the 'A' team remained unbeaten until January and eventually won the North London Thursday League. The Saturday 'A' team won the Islington League, despite having to play their home games at Fairlop in Essex. It was announced, however, that the junior teams would be scrapped for the following season and that the club would only compete against professional sides. In fact there is some evidence that the junior sides continued, but from now on they largely fall from view.

Further close season developments saw Harold Pitts (a young local player who had featured in many of the league matches) sign for Fulham, whilst the Islington Corinthians supporters held a Balloon Rally to help raise funds. Entry was one shilling and the balloon travelling the furthest distance would win a prize of ten shillings. In three years time there would have been some scope for cheating!

1934/35

The season opened with an invitation by Tom Smith for applications for membership from good amateur players, in an effort to improve on the previous season's performance. It was revealed later that Smith had received a large number of

19

applications. The opening game was just reward for Smith's close season efforts, as he fielded a team containing several internationals against Tufnell Park. A 2-0 victory was recorded against the Isthmian League club in a game held in aid of Hornsey Central Hospital.

The league programme did not get off to such a good start however, and West Ham United comfortably defeated the amateurs in the opening game. This result was avenged the following week as the I.C.'s stunned the professionals (after drafting in Fisher from the Royal Navy and the international Ling), with a 3-1 victory at Tufnell Park, and even had a goal disallowed. A strong Chelsea side brought the I.C.'s down to earth in the next league fixture, before Clapton Orient were held to a 1-1 draw when German international Helmuth Tirhih appeared for the amateurs.

It was now time to renew acquaintances with the Dutch champions Ajax who arrived in London the day prior to the match. The visitors were received at the Tufnell Park Hotel by Colonel A.W. Goodman, M.P., Alderman Bertie Holden, Alderman Manchester and Alderman Bull. Also in attendance was Mr S.F. Rous, secretary of the Football Association and Mr Hubard the F.A. Treasurer. The I.C.'s, as ever, entertained their guests royally, taking them to the Palladium the night before the game and, following the match, to the Empire Pool at Wembley to watch the Ice Hockey.

ISLINGTON CORINTHIANS 0 AJAX 6

'A disappointing attendance witnessed a game that was in marked contrast to the international match that was played a few hundred yards away the previous day. It was sporting in everyway. Sir F.J. Wall, who sat next to Col. A.W. Goodman, M.P., was a very interested spectator. Mr S.F. Rous and Leslie Knighton were also present.

A notable player on the Dutch side was G. Keizer, who will be remembered as an Arsenal goalkeeper a few seasons back. The Ajax party expressed themselves as being particularly delighted with their reception and entertainment since arriving in London.

The teams together with Sir F.J. Wall, Colonel Goodman, M.P., and Ald. Bertie Holden were photographed prior to the commencement of play. The players then lined up in the centre of the field to be presented to the three gentlemen mentioned.

Ajax had the advantage of the slope but Keizer was tested in the first minute. The Corinthians aggression was only momentary. The Dutchmen impressed with 'on the floor' passes and early proved themselves to be worthy opponents. Miller was wide when well place for opening the scoring. The ball ran awkwardly for Lister when the goal yawned.

Keizer collected the ball nicely and away Ajax went on the right. The ball went across and Wyngarden, who completely beat Smith to draw first blood for the Dutchmen. A fine run by Browne ended in Miller firing over. A shot by Volkers landed among the photographers to the merriment of the crowd. Smith was applauded for a spectacular save and later he cut out a ball that was entering the angle of crossbar and post.

A NARROW ESCAPE
An attack by the Ajax left ended in a post stopping a shot by Reenen adding to the Dutchmans score. At this period Ajax were definitely on top. There was more understanding and the Corinthians' defence had a hectic time. The Corinthians forced two quick corners, but Keizer was safe and confident. The first half was clearly in favour of Ajax, much of their football being quite good; whilst their sporting spirit was excellent.

Immediately upon resuming Ajax went further ahead, Have netting after a neat movement. Nottage was hurt too badly to resume, and Ted Hankins was allowed to take his place. Miller at last relieved the prolonged pressure on the Corinthians' goal with a fine run and shot, but quickly returning to the attack Ajax became three up, Van Reenan doing the trick with a splendid right-foot shot. Volkers scored number 4 for Ajax, who by now had proved themselves to be by far the superior side. Occasionally the Corinthians broke away but their finishing was poor.

The marking by the defence was bad. Volkers, who again netted, was unchallenged. Smith should have saved the next goal by Van Reenan but he allowed the ball to slip through his fingers. Ajax won 6-0 and were full value for their victory. It is not a pleasant reflection, that Englishmen were outclassed, as a team and surprised individually. Keizer did not have to negotiate a single shot that gave him serious trouble.'[15]

The result may have been unflattering, but the Islington Corinthians' time would come. Smith continued to get the best out of his team and they bounced back with a 4-2 win at home to Fulham. The following game against Chelsea was abandoned due to bad light, before a third league win was recorded against Park Royal.

The New Year saw the Islington Corinthians lose back to back games with Guildford City, but this was followed with a good win over the University of London. A 1-7 defeat to Arsenal, preceded either a 3-0 or 4-1 win over Tottenham Hotspur. Unfortunately press coverage of this game was poor, but it is known that C.G. Lungen of AFC (a Dutch second division team) appeared. Despite playing only at the second level, he was capped once by Holland. The season closed with a 2-1 win at Isthmian League Ilford, and an impressive 3-2 victory over Chelsea. The league table makes very satisfactory reading as the I.C.'s finished above both Fulham and Chelsea.

Left: The programme for Chelsea v Islington Corinthians on 28th November 1934

London Professional Midweek League					
	P	W	D	L	PTS
Dartford	12	7	2	3	16
Park Royal	12	6	2	4	14
Guildford City	12	6	2	4	14
West Ham United	12	5	3	4	13
Islington Corinthians	12	4	2	6	10
Fulham	12	3	3	6	9
Chelsea	12	3	2	7	8

It was not all good news, however, and the I.C's had their very own tragedy. It was reported:

*'On March 21st, Fred Hunter, aged 20, one of our juniors, in a match against Wallaces of Harlesden, broke his leg while playing. This unfortunate boy, whose mother is a widow, had now had to have his leg amputated. The club has passed round a subscription sheet to its players and supporters and we should be obliged if you could publish the list and also tender an appeal to the public who would like to subscribe.'*16

Hunter was by this point making a slow recovery in the Royal Northern Hospital, which had previously been supported by Islington Corinthian fundraising.

Despite the earlier heavy defeat at the hands of Ajax the Islington Corinthians were invited to visit Holland to coincide with England's visit on 18th May. As part of the arrangements, Ajax had secured tickets for the England game and would face the tourists the following day. The itinerary saw the party leave Liverpool Street at 8.30p.m. on Friday 17th May, and reach Amsterdam at 8a.m. on Saturday. They were to be met by the Amsterdam Rotary Club and be taken on a sightseeing trip of the city before watching the international.

The game versus Ajax ended in 3-1 victory for the touring side who featured an impressive team which included five internationals; the line up being S.R. Smith, F. Hicks, W. Shepherd, C. Saggers, B. Joy, K.H. Lister, E.C. Collins, W. Lockey, C. Lungen, J. Thompson, J. Browne. Bernard Joy was probably the most well-known and apart from being the last amateur to be awarded a full England cap, he was a famous Corinthian who won a league championship medal with Arsenal in 1937/38 season. Lister was also a Corinthian, whilst Lockey had appeared a number of times for the Casuals in the previous couple of seasons.

The following day the I.C.'s defeated a combined team from The Hague 3-2 in front of 4,000 spectators at the former ADO-stadium (Zuiderpark). On this occasion they needed to borrow a goal-keeper and got special permission to field their old friend Keizer. Islington took the lead in the fifth minute through Jones, before The Hague equalised. R.P. Tarrant making his first appearance for the club restored the lead after 17 minutes. Lister went on to make it 3-1 prior to the interval, and although The Hague rallied with the aid of the wind in the second half, they could only reduce the deficit by one goal.

There were a lot of congratulatory speeches at the annual dinner that followed the tour in June at Beale's Restaurant, and rightly so, as the club had continued to grow and had again collected its fair share of silverware in the form of the Hornsey Central Hospital Cup and the St. Dunstan's Shield.

Mr, Roston Bourke in proposing 'The Club,' said he knew of no better set of sportsmen than those to be found in Islington and he was convinced that the Islington Corinthians were going to revive in the Borough a deeper interest than ever in the amateur side of the game. Coupling with the toast the name of Mr. Tom Smith, the general hon. Secretary, the speaker paid warm tribute to his organising ability and wonderful energy.

CLUB'S PROGRESS REVIEWED
Mr. Smith, in reply, reviewed the progress made by the club since it inception three years ago. As sponsors they were fortunate in having the Islington Rotary Club. Mr. Smith went onto to refer to the fine spirit which animated the players, who were out to play football for football's sake. They had played more charity games than any amateur club he knew of, and had raised over £500 for charity.

The speaker said that the club had now got a really combined team that could give almost any team in London a good game. He went on to refer to the recent successful tour in Holland, where they beat Ajax by 3-1. A Dutch official paid them a handsome compliment when he said that Islington Corinthians were the finest amateur side seen in Holland for five years….

23

'This year we have sent a challenge to the Corinthians themselves,' said Mr. Smith who expressed the hope that they would come and see the class of football played by the Islington men and encourage them.

Also mentioned the Miss M. Smith – Tom's daughter who said 'the Islington Corinthians recognised ladies in their club far more than any other club she knew of.'[17]

1935/36

Islington Corinthians continued to make steady progress during their third season, and although no final league table is available, their record suggests that at the very least they repeated the previous season's third from bottom effort. The league season opened with a 1-3 defeat at home to Fulham, before an impressive 4-3 victory at Southend United secured the first points of the campaign.

The results were again inconsistent, and an 0-8 defeat to West Ham United (when the I.C.'s conceded six in the first 50 minutes) did not bode well for the rest of the season, but in the next match a late equaliser by Hannan rescued a point in a 4-4 draw with Tottenham Hotspur. The teams assembled by Tom Smith consisted of players borrowed from other amateur clubs in London, and this policy no doubt contributed to I.C.'s erratic performances.

Smith obviously had a bit more luck in the 2-0 victory over Q.P.R. as the Dutch international Lungen scored both goals in what was described as *'a nice, polite, sedate game with few thrills.'*[18] The last two games which can be traced prior to Christmas saw the I.C.'s crash 2-5 at home to Chelsea, (in a game enlivened by the referee being knocked out after being hit on the back of the head by a hard drive from L. Williams) and a 1-1 draw with Park Royal.

The Islington Corinthian newsletter at Christmas again highlighted how well the club was doing, and showed that there was a real club spirit developing as demonstrated by the injured players fund:

'Hullo Everybody, - The management of the Islington Corinthians Football Club wish to convey their appreciation and thanks to all who so nobly gave their support to the Jamboree held at Tufnell Park Hotel to provide a provident fund for injured players. We are very proud of these loyal associates who have made it possible for us to do our best for the boys. We are for sport and it is to our mind only right that those who 'take the kicks' should be safeguarded. We have a great regard for the lads who give of their best so that those of you who can, may enjoy the fare of the Club provides.

As an example of the great esteem in which we are held, I must point out that we always have the pleasure of high officials of the big League Clubs visiting us and paying us compliments. Now these gentlemen would not visit us and witness our games if they did not appreciate them, would they' [19]

The New Year opened with the Islington Corinthians recording a 3-1 win over Guildford City in the league, and after a two week break when Tom Smith went on holiday to Switzerland, the club faced Dartford. Dartford had recently found fame in the F.A. Cup when they went down narrowly by the odd goal in five to Derby County just a couple of weeks before this fixture. The I.C.'s performed well on the day and only lost 0-2 after conceding two goals in the dying minutes of the game.

After a couple of charity games where the Islington Corinthians played Wallace's in aid of Fred Hunter who, as mentioned, had lost his foot playing for the club, and the Post Office League for the St. Dunstan's Shield, (a game which raised the club's total charitable donations to more than £600), the I.C.'s lost 1-3 to Charlton Athletic. The last known result of the 1935/36 season was a creditable 1-1 draw with an Arsenal side that included both Dennis and Leslie Compton. It was a well contested game which could have gone either way, in front of one of the largest crowds at the park that year.
Following the Arsenal match the club held their second annual dinner at Beale's Assembly Rooms and the speeches give an indication of the feeling within the club at this point:

'The Secretary mentioned that the club had 104 first class amateur players; some were only able to turn out occasionally, but all went on the field with one idea – to play good football. 'I think we are the best losers of any amateur club in London.' Said Mr. Smith, who confessed that whilst they had suffered some really bad beatings, they had their bouts of success, and they had once had the pleasure of beating Chelsea. 'If the Arsenal are short of players in the final we shall be very pleased to supply them!' he jocularly observed.

.....As to future plans, he made it clear that they had no intention of starting Saturday matches, but had decided to stick to mid-week football. The club proposed to pay another visit to Holland in May.

'We are very proud of our charitable efforts,' he said. 'We have never refused a charity game. No matter whether on our own ground or not we are always willing to support any deserving charity.' 'I don't think a happier club exists,' added the secretary.' [20]

There are several indications that the club visited Holland, Belgium and Germany at the end of the season. In one source around the time of the world tour, it is stated that the club had previously defeated five of the strongest Dutch teams. The reliable rsssf.com website goes further to state that Sparta Rotterdam were defeated 1-0, whilst *The Times* discusses a W.S. Drake who went on an Islington Corinthian tour in 1936. Unfortunately there is very little evidence of what actually occurred and all that can be concluded is that it went very well.

CHAPTER TWO

THE ORIGINS OF THE TOUR 1936-1937

The Islington Corinthians were preparing for the new season, which again was to see them compete in the London Professional Midweek League, and to highlight the club's progress they had been invited to play in the prestigious London Challenge Cup with all of the capital's Football League clubs. At the end of August, however, the most important event in the club's short life occurred, one which was to change the whole course of the Islington Corinthians story. The Islington Gazette announced at the start of August that the Chinese Olympic team had been invited to play a game at Highbury, but interestingly did not mention their opponents. The opposition was confirmed shortly afterwards in their 12th August edition; not only were the Islington Corinthians to be given the honour of playing the tourists, but it was revealed that the club would field practically an international strength team.

Tom Smith had been active in the close season and had attracted an impressive list of recruits for the forthcoming campaign. The Casuals, winners of the F.A. Amateur Cup the previous season, supplied A.H. Fabian, L.T. Huddle and their free scoring centre forward B.A. Clements. John Sutcliffe (Corinthian), L.C. Thornton (Kingstonian), F. Stein (Belgium), H.E. Barnes (Wimbledon), G. Sargent and J. Osbourne (Romford) were also now I.C.'s and together formed the strongest playing membership the club had enjoyed thus far. Smith was also attempting to raise the profile of the club in the local area and made the following appeal for support:

'Mr. Tom Smith, the indefatigable Hon. Secretary, wants the business and professional men of Islington to join up as patron members. For a guinea they can watch all home League and Friendly matches at Tufnell Park in a comfortable grandstand seat. Ladies may have the same privileges for 7s 6d per annum.'[1]

The excitement built up in the next three weeks until the arrival of the Chinese, fresh from a 2-2 draw with Red Star Paris, (one of the strongest professional sides in France and winners of the French Cup a record four times) and a crowd of 30 to 40,000 was anticipated. This would be the first Chinese side to play in England, and Arsenal

26

entertained them at their home game with Everton on the previous Saturday, before the tourists were taken on the Sunday to Hampton Court and Windsor.

Smith was concentrating on assembling the strongest side he could muster and with an ever keen eye for publicity, even tried to get permission for Arsenal's Alex James and Cliff Bastin to appear in the game, despite being professionals. The F.A. refused this request but it did not prevent Smith's Islington Corinthians from fielding a formidable team. The outstanding L.T. Huddle would appear between the sticks, whilst in front of him was an impressive array of amateur talent; G.S. Burchell, R. Ellis, S. Eastham, E. Tunnington, J. Sutcliffe, E. Collins, J.W. Lewis, J. Osbourne, W. Sparks and finally Barnet legend L. Finch. The F.A. completed the all star line up by naming F.A. Cup final referee, Mr H. Nattrass, to officiate in the middle.

ISLINGTON CORINTHIANS 3 CHINA 2

'Last evening the Arsenal club had the pleasure of introducing to a London crowd China's artistic and nimble Soccer football team, several of whom had taken part in the recent Olympic Games at Berlin. Our visitors had for opposition a strong side of the Islington Corinthians, who played seven amateur internationals.

Clothed in blue and white and terminating their sartorial get-up with flaming red stockings, the young men of China – average age about 25 – stood gravely in line opposite their foes while the two national national anthems were played, and the music had scarcely died away when the Tourists amazed the crowd by opening the score.

TWO UP IN 20 MINUTES
The movement was so amazingly clever in its combination that one soon began to realise why China had run England so close in Berlin. Their early success, moreover, was capped inside the first 20 minutes, when the centre-forward, with admired coolness, trapped the ball and scored one of the best goals I have seen in some years.

These dapper fellows know how to shoot, and they understand also the art of finding their men with neat butterfly touches.

The Corinthians eventually won – their goals fell to Tunnington, Osbourne and Lewis – but they had to go all the way and discovered in Ke Leang Fung a goal keeper of exceptional merit.

Perhaps it was the fantastic names of the Chinese team that put the Britishers off the mark. They ought not to have read the programme: it was full of strange hyphenated names that spoke of mystery and magic.

Witness for instance, the men who scored China's two goals: King Cheung Fung and Wai-Tong Lee; also their best back, Bon-lay Chua.

Above Left: Wai Tong Lee (Capt. Chinese XI) & E. Tunnington (Capt. Islington Corinthians) greeted by the Mayor of Islington before the match.

Above Right: Action shot from Islington Corinthians v Chinese Olympic XI

Some of the Chinese team are in commercial life; two are policemen; another is an army instructor – but they are all clever footballers. Their heading was particularly good – better still the forwards kept the ball studiously on the ground.

ONLY A RESERVE!
The team played according to our English style, with the centre-half lying well back and the centre-forward nearly as far up, and though faltering during the middle of the second half, they made a great though vain rally near the end.

China's goalkeeper was a reserve player, if you please' but he had the skill and alacrity to grace the best of our English teams, and the Corinthians, though shooting badly at various periods gave him lots of chances.'[2]

It was a tremendous achievement for the club but, strangely, following this match interest in the Islington Gazette waned, except for discussions on the world tour. The only two results which are mentioned for the season were a 1-2 London Challenge Cup defeat at Southall in the preliminary round and a 2-7 defeat at Folkestone in the I.C.'s opening league fixture. The league fixtures would have included matches against Fulham reserves, Southend United, (managed by David Jack), Clapton Orient and Guildford City.

Organising the World Tour

Following the game with the Chinese the Islington Corinthians were invited to play in China, and Tom Smith's mind went into overdrive about this tremendous opportunity. Smith recalled the sequence of events:

'It is all due to a series of incidents which happened a year ago. My daughter who is keen on sports, went to the Olympic Games and on her return suggested to me that the American football team be asked to go to England. Usually when a team visits England it is those managing who have to dig pretty deeply into their pockets. However, while there she was greatly impressed by the Chinese football team. Englishmen admire pluck and perseverance and she was struck by the fact that the Chinese team had fought their way across the world to play football in Europe.

When the Chinese team played in England on the Arsenal ground, Mr. Allison, the Arsenal manager, said that the Arsenal themselves had learned something by the way the Chinese played. Beside being good footballers they proved themselves good sports and gentlemen. We got to know them and we admired them, and it was really a great pleasure to take them around. They did appreciate what little we did for them. After their departure back to their own country, it was the suggestion of Mr. Wong Ke-tsun that an English side go out East. I thought it a joke. But Mr. Wong after some great thought asked me why not go out the same way as the Chinese had done and work their way. It did not seem feasible at the time, but after 12 months of work, I got a scheme together.'[3]

Smith started work almost immediately and between the 31st August 1936, when the I.C.'s had beaten China, and November he had made the preliminary moves which ultimately led to the tour becoming a reality. Smith had already managed to attract criticism in the national press, which clearly did not share his vision, but this did not distract him from his goal. The Islington Gazette reported on the 18th November that plans for the world tour were progressing well and that matches would be played in eleven countries, with the tour starting in November 1937.

By December, Smith was in a position to disclose the initial details to the press, but he emphasised that there were still many difficulties to overcome:

'The Islington Corinthians' world tour is taking shape but there are difficulties in Mr. Tom Smith's path. Although the guarantees in India and China have been satisfactorily arranged, he has still to get the majority of the players.

As the tour will last from November, 1937 to May, 1938, it may be hard to find 20 or so players of amateur international standard who could afford to take such a long time off. George Sargeant, Romford full-back, who gave such an excellent performance for the Football Association against the Navy on Wednesday, will be able to go.

Corporal S. Eastham, Army and amateur international right-half, and perhaps other players who will be leaving the various Services next spring also will go. Charlton Athletic have agreed to release Hicks, and Mr. Smith thinks that Fulham may release Parry.

The tour is very attractive. Seeing the world and playing football in India, Ceylon, China, Japan, Canada, etc., is fine but many men Tom would like to take cannot get away for six months at a stretch.'[4]

One can but wonder at the roller-coaster of emotions Smith probably experienced when organising the world tour. In Smith's own words, they started without a friend in the world, but overcame opposition in the press, the clubs who were losing their players for an entire season and the Football Association. Smith spoke in Malaya about his task in arranging such a massive voyage:

'Mr. Smith said that to most people it would appear that taking a football team round the world would just mean getting together a team, fixing up a few matches, having plenty of people to watch the team play, going out into the world and letting members of the team thoroughly enjoy themselves.

Speaking from his own experience, he found that taking a football side round the world meant an amazing amount of work. When he first decided to take a team on such a trip, he met with tremendous opposition.

It was suggested to him that it would be impossible to get a team who would be prepared to be away for eight months and give an exhibition of English amateur football, that probably the team would be stranded after going half way round the world, due to shortage of funds, and that the worst prospect of such a trip would be that the side would let down English amateur soccer by being badly beaten.

'In the first instance, the Football Association flatly turned down the suggestion,' Mr. Smith went on. 'After a time, I submitted all my plans and arrangements. The Association people then altered their minds, and here we are.'

'We started out without a friend in the world.'

...'You have got to be a super-optimist before going on such a trip,' he said. 'First of all, you must imagine that your team is going to be a big attraction abroad, but when you get to foreign countries and find that the people are disinclined to turn up at the matches the team plays, you must not be disheartened. For instance, when I first arrived here I was told that rugger is the game, and I was asked why I did not bring a good rugger team out.'

'Apart from the question of finance, there was the risk of accidents, epidemics and sickness among the players. Then there was the question of making arrangements for

travel. Delays in shipping arrivals or in train departures would sometimes upset all calculations.'[5]

By April, Tom Smith was ready to face the stiff upper lipped Football Association and ask for their approval of the world tour. Permission was by no means guaranteed, but Smith somehow managed to convince the F.A. that it was a worthwhile exercise, and that the funds were in place to ensure that the trip did not end in disaster.

Smith recalled the meeting with the Football Association later in the trip:
'We offered to back the scheme financially, but they (the F.A.) turned it down. All they turned down was the fact that they did not want their name in the scheme. Before anything was decided we had to submit plans and finances arranged before they would make up their minds. I travelled to London for the meeting of the Football Association and there submitted my plans. One of your members Mr. Stokes was there, but I was not introduced to him. I introduced myself across the table. Mr. Stokes agreed that the Corinthians would be very welcome out East and after two hours of cross-examination, the Chairman of the Association came to me and said that mine was a pioneer effort and wished me success.'[6]

The Islington Gazette covered the meeting giving the basic details in the days following the discussions:

'A special committee of the F.A. received Mr. Tom Smith, the Hon. Secretary and Mr Sleight, the Chairman of Islington Corinthians to hear full details of the club's proposed world tour.

The committee – H.J. Huband, W.W. Heard, and Mark Frowde – informed him that he will hear later whether or no the scheme has their blessing.

Mr. Smith, we understand, put his case very fully and convincingly. They have the money and the men, and the O.K. should be forthcoming.

We trust for Mr. Smith's sake and the club's sake that this big undertaking will be a great success.'[7]

With permission received, Smith then had just five months to assemble a team capable of facing the best teams in the countries that were to be visited. This was never going to be an easy task, as he would have to find players potentially willing to leave their families for eight months and to arrange time off of work for those in employment. This problem was to plague Smith until almost the last moment as he struggled to finalise the list of players who would be making the trip. In July the following twenty players were named as the Islington Corinthians tour party: E. Winfield (Romford), C. Longman (Kingstonian), Pat Clark (Leyton), G. Sargent (Romford), A.J. Martin (Tunbridge Wells Rangers), J.K. Wright (Wimbledon), R.E. Banks (Moor Green), W. Whittaker (Kingstonian), G. Howlett (Romford), S. Eastham (Army), J. Braithwaite

(Barnet), L. Bradbury (Moor Green), L.C. Thornton (Derby Amateurs), R. Tarrant (Sutton United), C. Lungen (Dutch International), H.E.R. Barnes (Wimbledon), G.W.E. Pearce (Hoxton Manor), J. Miller (Dulwich Hamlet), L. Stone (Woking) and J. Sherwood (Reading).

In the next two months six players would withdraw from the squad, and Smith would need to try and find replacements for them with practically no notice. Fortunately, Smith had strong backing and his efforts were availing as he later recalled:

'Employers had been extremely kind in granting players leave of absence and giving most of them half pay and in a few cases full pay. Only one refusal from an employer was received.'[8]

The players invited were most enthusiastic about the trip, and some were willing to take the risk of leaving their jobs. The captain Pat Clark stated *'Some have thrown up jobs to be with us on this trip,'*[9] giving an indication that not everything was as easy as Smith recounts.

One player to miss out was the international Stanley Eastham of Kingstonian, who was a corporal in the King's Own Royal Regiment and had captained the Army and Aldershot Command. He would have been a tremendous addition to the tour party, having played in all the England Amateur Internationals in 1936 and been selected for the 1936 Great Britain Olympic squad. Eastham had gained numerous other honours and was taken on the F.A. tour to New Zealand in the Summer of 1937. Unfortunately for Eastham he still had two months left in the army and could not get further leave (especially in view of his recent return from New Zealand). Despite being keen to go, he was unable to gain a release and was considering turning professional with rumours that Arsenal and Liverpool were both interested in signing him. In May 1938 he was to sign for Liverpool. In any event it opened the door for W. Miller who took his place on the tour.

One of the most pertinent questions is; how did the Islington Corinthians fund their world tour? Smith was a resourceful soul and noted that *'the Chinese team made nearly £3,000 profit on their world tour, and this was utilised to defray the expenses of the athletes who came from China to the Olympic Games.'*[10] This is all very positive, but the fact remained that the I.C.'s world tour was going to cost £12,000. To put this figure in perspective, in 1937 a four bedroom house in Islington could be bought for £410. It was therefore a significant amount of money, but again Smith used his Rotarian contacts to ensure this would be forthcoming. *'Mr. Smith mentioned that Lt. Com. Tufnell, M.P. (Vice-President of the Islington Corinthians F.C.) had sent a cheque for £200, expressing his warm approval of the tour because of the friendly feeling that was promoted between the different countries by means of sport'*[11]

Above: The Islington Corinthians
Back Row: W. Duke, R.P. Tarrant, H.C. Read, E. Wingfield, G. Dance, C. Longman, C.F.S. Slight (Chairman), A.J. Martin, L. Bradbury, A. Suter

Front Row: A.D. Buchanan, P.B. Clark (Captain), J.K. Wright, J.W. Sherwood, L.G. Stone, T. Smith (Hon. Sec. & Manager), H. Lowe (Trainer), G.W.E. Pearce, J.C. Braithwaite, J.W. Miller, E. Gardiner

Smith revealed on the I.C.'s return from the tour that: *'Finance was a great problem, but thanks to his personal friends, members of the Islington Rotary Club, and Lt. Commander Tufnell, the obstacle was finally overcome. Commander Studd, one of their vice-presidents guaranteed all their travelling expenses, and was so pleased with the results of the tour that he had offered to do so again should they embark on a similar venture in the future.'*[12] Smith had covered every eventuality and would have been confident that the guarantees he had arranged with the various governing bodies of the countries to be visited and the percentages of the gate money would more than cover their expenses.

When more advanced details were announced in July the expectation was that Islington Corinthians would start their tour in France, against Racing Club de Paris. This fixture was replaced at the very last moment by three games in Holland but the following planned arrangements remained essentially intact. In October the I.C.'s would visit Switzerland, before travelling to Egypt. They would next spend six weeks in India, until the New Year, when they would proceed down through Burma to Malaya and from there to Manila in the Philippine Islands. Hong Kong, Shanghai and Japan, (where four games would be played) would complete the Asian leg of the tour. From Japan the team would visit Honolulu, then travel on to games in the United States and

Canada, before returning home. The changing world political scene obviously impacted on this itinerary, but nevertheless the very ambitious programme was largely fulfilled.

Tom Smith was now ready to address his backers, the Islington Rotarians, and during a speech in September 1937, he summarised the club's plans:

'Mr. Smith, went onto indicate the innumerable difficulties which were then encountered in making the necessary arrangements. Getting into touch with the football authorities of the various countries to be included in the tour was by no means a simple matter, and having established contact, there were all kinds of negotiations as to guarantees, etc., to be conducted. Then there was the financing of the tour, and the securing of the Football Association's permission to run the tour, whilst employers had to be consulted with a view to the players being granted seven months' leave of absence. In the latter connection Mr. Smith said that employers generally, and educational authorities in particular, had been exceptionally fine.

Mr. Smith added that practically every hurdle had now been overcome and a trial match for the purpose of selecting players for the tour had been held on the previous evening.

The Islington Corinthians would be leaving London early next month 22 to 24 strong, and they would begin their tour by going to Paris where they would meet the Racing Club of Paris, who played the Arsenal every year. Switzerland would be the next country to be visited, and at Berne they would have the experience of opening a new sports stadium and playing a match by flood-lighting. Next they would move to Marseilles and then from Genoa to Egypt, where they expected to encounter some stiff opposition in games at Alexandra and Cairo.

On arrival in India, they would have a big programme in front of them, embracing some 24 matches in 50 days, including a game with the Army team on the North-West frontier, and other matches at Lahore, Delhi and Calcutta. Then onto Burma, where two matches would be played at Rangoon, continuing on to Penang in the Straits. The programme made provision for eight games in Malaya, leaving Singapore on January 28th. From there the plans are somewhat indefinite at the moment owing to the unsettled conditions in the Far East, but there would be a two weeks' stay in Hong Kong, and it was also hoped to include French Cochin China and Java in the itinerary. The Philippine Islands had asked to be included in the tour, whilst it was intended to visit Honolulu, and then proceed on to San Francisco and up to Vancouver, returning across Canada to play games at Calgary, Toronto and Montreal.

Mr. Smith mentioned that the party would be taking with them a full-size film camera to take a pictorial record of the tour.

Rotarian Baldwin, in voicing the Club's thanks to the speaker, conveyed their best wishes to the Islington Corinthians for a very successful tour and said how much they would be missed at Tufnell Park. He stressed the value of such tours in cementing friendship between the nations.'[13]

Smith again had one eye on the future and the idea of filming the trip was ahead of its time. Unfortunately the film never seems to have been made, and the assumption must be that the project was abandoned with the outbreak of war in 1939. The same is likely to have happened to the book which was meant to have been written about the events and experiences of the tour by Mrs Searles, a journalist who accompanied the tourists. Had these both been produced, perhaps the Islington Corinthians would not have been forgotten by football historians.

The tour was now finalised and all that was left for the I.C.'s was to prepare for the forthcoming trip with several friendly matches. The Islington Corinthians produced some good displays in beating Fulham 3-1 at Craven Cottage, and succumbing only to a goal five minutes from time in a 1-2 defeat against West Ham United. Tour captain Pat Clark scored a stunning free kick for the amateurs in the latter game. The final warm up match in early September was interesting in that although the world tour was just weeks away, the club chose to visit Holland. The visitors recorded a 4-3 victory over Blau-Wit, despite being three goals in arrears with just fifteen minutes remaining.

CHAPTER THREE

WHO WERE THE TOURISTS?

During the Summer of 1937, Tom Smith had been actively trying to gather a squad of players to represent the Islington Corinthians on their world tour. It would have been impossible for the players not to realise what was happening in the world at this point as the storm clouds were gathering rapidly. The tour itinerary in itself would have been enough to deter the fainthearted as it was proposed that the team would play in Shanghai, which was a war zone, and Japan who were the expansionist aggressors in the region.

At home Britain's policy of appeasement under Neville Chamberlain's leadership merely legitimised Hitler's plans for a Nazi super state embracing the entire German volk. From the point when Hitler and the Nazi Party came to power in 1933, there had been a steady flow of warning signs as to what Hitler's intentions were. In 1935 the Saarland was reunited with Germany, whilst controversially Hitler ordered his army to reoccupy the Rhineland in March 1936 in direct violation of the Versailles Treaty. Six months later Italy and Germany had signed a treaty of friendship which was the start of a more formal co-operation between the two dictatorships. The Islington Corinthians players would therefore have embarked on their world tour unsure of what might confront them on their return. With hindsight it is easy to see how war was inevitable by 1937, but how apparent would it have been to the players involved? It would surely have been obvious that the heightened tension in world politics was approaching a climax, and that the future course of events largely depended on how far the British government was prepared to go to accomodate Hitler's expansionist vision.

As it was Tom Smith was successful in gathering enough players to make the voyage, but there must have been some apprehension in regard to the Shanghai and Tokyo leg of the journey. Japan and China had not enjoyed good relations since 1931 when the Japanese invaded Manchuria as a result of the Mukden Incident. In July 1937, just months before the Islington Corinthians were due to depart, the Second Sino-Japanese War erupted and between August and November full scale fighting ensued across Northern China including the Battle of Shanghai. On the Saturday before the club's departure *The Times* headlines ran: *'Japan as aggressor'* and *'Japan rejects mediation – 'Fight to bitter end.''* This would have left no illusions as to what they were walking into.

Trouble in the region began to be covered regularly by the press in July 1937 and an early indication of future problems was reported in *The Times* in the 2nd July edition, which stated that Russian and Japanese forces had clashed on the Amur River in China. Ten days later *The Times* stated that war between Japan and China was inevitable, and tension continued to rise until on the 21st July the headlines ran: *'Fighting in China.'*

By the end of July, the war in China was a regular news item as the heavy fighting continued with the Japanese using the tactic of bombing towns and cities into submission. On the 16th August the *The Times* reported that 1,000 people had been killed in Shanghai and that the city had been devastated by Chinese bombs as they attempted to recapture the city and drive out the Japanese.

It was shortly after this that the world realised that Japan was seeking total victory over China and was in a position to deploy two million troops to achieve that goal. Shanghai was burning and in September the Japanese advised all foreigners to evacuate Shanghai as they were expecting more air raids by the Chinese air force.

Diplomatic efforts were failing and Japan rejected mediation offers by the League of Nations. The British government was now anxious and the British ambassador in Tokyo was ordered to protest to the Japanese government in regard to the bombing of non military targets which had killed numerous civilians. Five days before the tourists departed *The Times* headline ran: *'Japan Shocks the World'* as Japan had sunk a Chinese fishing fleet without warning, killing all but a handful of the crews.

Despite all the news which was readily available to the tourists the schedule remained unchanged, and Shanghai and Tokyo would remain on the fixture list. With six months to go before the tourists were due to arrive it must have been hoped that by then hostilities would have ceased. Curiously there is no evidence to suggest that the Foreign Office or the Football Association, who had full details of the tour and had sanctioned it, made any efforts to prevent the Islington Corinthians from visiting these countries.

The war in China was to rumble on until 1941 when it was enveloped by the world war, but fortunately for the tourists fighting had moved away from the Shanghai area by the time of their arrival, and the city was firmly controlled by the Japanese. During the period that the tourists were away, the situation worsened on the home front with the annexation of Austria by Germany in March 1938, and at this point Hitler turned his attention to the Sudetenland region of Czechoslovakia. A year after their return the players would be faced with the prospect of enlistment as Britain was at war.

Perhaps the players were willing to accept the risks of a season-long journey round the world precisely because of the uncertainty created by Germany, the tour being viewed as a last hurrah before the inevitable war occurred. Perhaps, more altruistically, they saw themselves as goodwill ambassadors seeking to improve international relations by sporting contacts. The fact remains that war was a distinct possibility and with it the probable conscription of most young, fit and able men into the services. Careers would then take second place regardless of whether the indiviuals went on the tour or not.

Who were the players?

Who were the Islington Corinthians tourists? Who were these gifted amateur footballers that Tom Smith persuaded to throw in their lot in England and make the trip of a lifetime? Smith had managed against the odds to assemble a talented team from the leading southern and midland clubs, in addition to a strong supporting cast in the form of Miss Starr (his secretary), Mrs Searles (a journalist who was intending to write a book about the ground breaking trip) and Harry Lowe (the coach). Now it is time to introduce what turned out to be a wonderful cast of characters and gentlemen.

Horace 'Harry' Lowe

The coach Harry Lowe was born in Northwich on 10th August 1886, and was adopted as a child. He began his playing career with his home town club, playing in the powerful Lancashire Combination against the likes of Accrington Stanley, Barrow and Tranmere Rovers. In 1913 he was signed by Brighton and Hove Albion from Northwich Victoria as a forward, and was then transformed into a centre half. In April 1914 he transferred to Tottenham Hotspur for £75 before his playing career was rudely interrupted by the outbreak of war, during which he served in the Tank Corps. Prior to the suspension of football, he had time to make his Football League debut, against Middlesbrough on 13th February 1915.

After the war he returned to Tottenham and in all made 65 appearances before transferring to Fulham for £250 in May 1927. Lowe made just three appearances for Fulham in his one season at Craven Cottage and then played for Beckenham, before beginning his coaching career. He first accepted a job offer in Spain coaching Deportivo Espanyol and later moved to Real Sociedad who were known at this point as Donostia San Sebastion, but was forced to return to England in 1935, due to the looming Spanish Civil War. It has been rumoured that Lowe played for Real Sociedad against Valencia on 24th March 1935 aged 44 years, but if this is the same Harry Lowe he would have been 48 years old.

Lowe's career took a new turn when he became coach of the Islington Corinthians (by 1937) and following the world tour he returned to Tottenham as coach and reserve team manager. After World War Two he managed Bournemouth and Yeovil Town for two years. Harry died in Camden Town on 15th July 1966.

Alfred Victor Avery (Sonny)

Sonny Avery was a 22 year old professional cricketer with Essex County Cricket Club at the time of the trip and he managed to fit in the majority of the voyage around the cricketing season. Sonny was born on 19th December 1914 in New Beckton, Essex and was destined to be an accomplished all round sportsman. In football he was an inside forward and was famed for his astute dribbling and inexhaustible energy. He played for Athenian League club Leyton who had been making a name for themselves with five appearances in the F.A. Amateur Cup final since 1927 (winning twice). Sonny appeared in the latest of these memorable matches, the 1937 final where Leyton faced the mighty Dulwich Hamlet. Sonny had scored the equaliser against Sutton United in the semi final, and was destined to hit the post in the final, as Leyton succumbed 0-2 in front of 30,000 supporters. Avery had accumulated many representative honours including a county cap.

He was however better remembered for his cricket where, in a first class career spanning 19 years (1935-1954), he played in 268 matches for Essex, scoring 14,045 runs in 453 innings, including 25 centuries. Sonny played at a time when Essex relied heavily on amateur players, who were not always available and they became known as a dangerous if inconsistent side. As a result, Sonny was denied the cricketing honours his talent deserved.

Leonard Bradbury

Len Bradbury who was born in Northwich in 1914, was one of two midlands based players selected for the tour, and played for the famous amateur club Moor Green. In 1936 whilst studying at Manchester University he gained his solitary cap when he was selected for the England amateur international side which defeated Ireland 5-0 at Blackpool. His other honours included being selected for the British Universities team which went to the 1935 international student games. Len was described as a very intellectual inside forward and was 23 years old at the time of the tour. Bradbury was still a student at this point, and was in the fortunate position of being able to take a break from his studies, without having commitments elsewhere or having to leave a job. Len's other clubs included Northwich Victoria, Corinthians, Birmingham University and Manchester United for whom he played two games, scoring one goal during the 1938/39 season.

Jack C. Braithwaite
The 25 year old Jack Braithwaite was one of Smith's acquisitions from Barnet F.C., one of the top Athenian League clubs. Braithwaite returned from Tufnell Park in time for the 1936/37 season and enjoyed an impressive return of 15 goals. He scored a hat-trick in the Herts Charity Cup final, enabling Barnet to retain the trophy, but missed out on both Barnet's near misses in the Athenian League (runners-up) and F.A. Amateur Cup (semi finalists), while he was away on tour. He had impressed enough to be awarded a county cap for Hertfordshire. Braithwaite was an Insurance Official by profession, and doubled as a Dance Band leader, which explains why he was always ready to get involved in the musical exploits of the team whilst on tour.

Alec D. Buchanan (Alec)
Alec Buchanan who was born in Scotland, was another 25 year old player from Barnet F.C. where he played 32 games during the 1936/37 season and the first three games of the following season prior to the world tour. He received his full colours from London University between the years 1931 and 1933 and also appeared for Chelsea. On his return from the tour Buchanan played for Nunhead and was capped by Surrey.

Pat B. Clark

Pat Clark was another Scottish player selected for the Islington Corinthians having been born in Rosewell, Midlothian. Pat was no stranger to touring, having previously been selected for the Middlesex Wanderers although *'Clark recalled as a child playing a game 25 miles from his town and that being a journey into the unknown.'*[1] Clark was destined to better this by 6,000 miles.

Following his time spent at Edinburgh University, where he captained their football team and gained full Blues between 1929 and 1932, he moved to London to become a schoolmaster and joined Leyton F.C., whom he later captained. In 1937, he appeared alongside Sonny Avery in their F.A. Amateur Cup final defeat by Dulwich Hamlet. It was a game he would probably rather forget as he missed an easy chance late in the game to put Leyton back in contention.

Clark's football career had seen him appear for Hibernian and Brentford, as well as being named reserve for the Scotland versus England amateur international of 1932. Pat obtained further representative honours when he was selected for the Athenian League and London F.A. teams. Following the world tour he joined Dick Tarrant at Sutton United, where he played until the war. Clark's playing style as full back was described as fearless and rugged.

George W. Dance

George Dance was the second of two Moor Green players selected by Tom Smith and was the oldest playing member of the tour party at 29 years of age. Dance was a Correspondence Clerk by profession, but it was as a right half or centre half that he really made his mark. He played in the 1933 international trial match at Wolverhampton and was later capped by the Birmingham and District Amateur Association for games against Worcestershire, Gloucestershire and the London F.A. Dance's greatest honour was being selected to play for an F.A. XI.

Cyril Longman

Cyril was a very promising goal keeper who, by the age of 22, had already won a first team place in the powerful Kingstonian team and helped them to an Isthmian League championship during the 1936/37 season. Longman was a very agile keeper and prior to the world tour it was reported: *'The prospect of filling Longman's place so easily and satisfactorily is not so rosy. He has set a standard of goalkeeping which G. Lindsey, the new man from Hersham, will not find it simple to reach.'*[2] Kingstonian were to feel his loss and disappointed in the ensuing season.

Longman's career was badly interrupted by the war, although he did gain a Surrey County Badge having played for them on three occasions. After the war he appeared during the 1945/46 season for St. Albans City. Cyril was a carpenter by trade.

Richard L. Manning

Dick Manning was something of an oddity in that of all the players selected by Tom Smith, he alone did not play for any of the famous amateur clubs. It is not known if he had appeared for the Islington Corinthians prior to the world tour, but his selection from little known Clacton Town was somewhat out of keeping with the illustrious list of internationals and amateur cup finalists who were making the trip. Manning was clearly acquainted with some of the players making the trip, although the connection is unknown, as W. Miller and R.P. Tarrant both guested for Clacton in the month leading up to the tour.

Clacton Town had been runners up in the Eastern Counties League in 1936/37, before transferring to the ill fated Essex League for one year. Manning started the season with Clacton, appearing in a 0-4 league drubbing by Harwich & Parkeston, and friendly defeats at the hands of Barnet, Q.P.R. and Chelmsford. The local Clacton Times, was delighted with the inclusion of three players in the Islington Corinthians party, although two of them are unlikely to have pulled on a Clacton jersey had it not been for the tour! *'A high honour indeed for Clacton football to have three men selected for*

41

international football. We can ill-afford to spare them, but I know everyone associated with Clacton F.C. will wish them well.'[3]

Alfred J. Martin

Eddy Martin as he was known was a 28 year old amateur with Southern League Tunbridge Wells Rangers, having previously spent time playing in the French first division with Antibes where he was captain during the 1931/32 season. Martin was a popular figure at Tunbridge Wells, and it was reported: *'It is to be regretted that A.J. Martin, who played so many fine games as an amateur for the club last season, will not be available, but he will be on a round-the-world tour with Islington Corinthians.'*[4] He did however start the season with them and played in the impressive victories over Exeter City, Swindon Town and Torquay United.

During the war, whilst awaiting his call-up, he occupied himself by making fighting Frenchmen feel at home in England. Probably through contacts he made during this activity, he played for the Free French football team and scored their only goal in a game against the National Fire Service. At this time he was broadcasting regularly to France on behalf of the B.B.C.

Martin was the only married member of the tour party, and left behind his small family when he made the trip. He was in a good position to provide for them as he owned a garage in New Cross. During his life he also owned a circus in Margate, which burned down.

John William Miller

 Johnny Miller was a fast, two footed winger, who was born in Leyton on 12th September 1912. He had a long and successful career as an amateur footballer, starting out at Tufnell Park, whom he played for until the Summer of 1936 when he joined Dulwich Hamlet. In the 1936/37 season Miller played 23 games for Hamlet, scoring three goals during their F.A. Amateur Cup winning season, although he did not appear in the final. In this season Miller was also selected to represent the Middlesex F.A. and the Isthmian League.

On his return from the world tour, Miller joined Fulham, where he made four first team appearances during the 1938/39 season, although he moved to St. Albans City before the end of the campaign. His spell at St. Albans City was to straddle the war and he was to make 55 appearances for them, scoring seven goals, the last being during the 1945/46 season.

By 1947, Johnny had joined Margate and made an immediate impression when he scored direct from a corner kick on his debut away at Lloyds in a Kent League fixture. By the end of the season he had made 18 appearances for Margate, scoring eleven times. The following season Johnny made another 25 appearances, scoring eight goals, and at this point he intended to retire and play only when the team was desperate. This did not quite materialise as Miller was to play in 30 games and add another nine goals to his Margate total. Miller was finally allowed to retire quietly during the 1950/51 season when he made just two appearances.

Johnny's professional career saw him work in the newsreel business, and the plan was for him to shoot a film of the trip. Regrettably this never came to fruition. Johnny died in 1990.

William Miller

Bill Miller was a member of the Dulwich Hamlet F.A. Amateur Cup winning side of 1934. However, it is unlikely that he remembered much about the final, having been badly concussed following a clash of heads, and Dulwich eventually clung on for victory despite only having seven fit players at the final whistle.

Miller had begun his football with Hayes, before transferring to Dulwich in 1933, and having the unenviable task of filling the boots of the legendary Edgar Kail at inside right. This was no easy task considering that, although an amateur, Kail had been capped three times for the full England side in 1929 in the games against Spain, Belgium and France.

Bill made 26 appearances, scoring ten goals, for Dulwich during the 1933/34 season and the following season played 13 games, scoring two goals. At the end of the season he joined Wimbledon. Miller also gained representative honours when he was selected for the Isthmian League, the Middlesex F.A. and F.A. XI teams. He also appeared for Charlton Athletic as an amateur. Miller was once described as a long striding player, with fine ball control and an accurate shot.

George W.E. Pearce
George Pearce was a player Tom Smith acquired from Hoxton Manor, a team in the Spartan League which subsequently amalgamated with Crown F.C., to become Crown & Manor during World War Two. Crown & Manor went on to play for many years in the various incarnations of the Spartan League after a spell in the Parthenon League. Whilst at Hoxton Manor, George represented the London F.A. and Middlesex F.A. and on his return went on to play for Barking. He was described in his tour profile as an export clerk.

H.C. Read
Bert Read was a 25 year old player with Nunhead, the famous Surrey side which had consecutive Isthmian League championship wins in 1928/29 and 1929/30. Read

played for the club from 1934 to 1939 as a winger and helped his club to runners-up position during the 1936/37 campaign. During the 1935/36 season Read was a member of the team which played against Watford in the F.A. Cup first round, losing 2-4. Bert's other exploits with Nunhead saw him included in the two touring sides that visited Dieppe at Easter 1936 and 1937. Read represented Surrey four times and was a Commercial Traveller by profession.

Henry William Sherwood

Johnny Sherwood had the most eventful life of anyone who made the trip. He was born on 3rd September 1913 into a local Reading family known as 'the Showbiz Sherwoods,' five brothers who were a popular mime act before World War Two. Johnny opted for football rather than the family calling and was a promising youngster with Maidenhead United and then Reading when he was selected to go on the world tour, where he led the Islington Corinthians' scoring charts.

Following the world tour he rejoined Reading and scored on his league debut, but was generally used as a wing half in most of the games he played. Sherwood continued to play for Reading during the early part of World War Two and scored the first goal in Reading's London War Cup triumph in 1941.

Sherwood's life then took a new twist in 1942 when he was captured by the Japanese and forced to work on the notorious Burma railway of death, ironically a place he had enjoyed just five years before. Thanks to Johnny's fitness he managed to survive for three and a half years, before being shipped to Japan. It was during this voyage that the ship carrying him was torpedoed and sunk, leaving him having to spend three days in shark infested waters, before being rescued by the enemy and being taken to Nagasaki where he was to witness the dropping of the atom bomb.

After the war Sherwood returned to his football career and played two more games for Reading, against the two clubs he went onto play for; Aldershot and Crystal Palace. Following these games he never regained his first team spot, but did finish top scorer of the reserves in the 1946/47 season. Sherwood's final record for Reading stood at nine Football League appearances and one goal, as well as 26 war time games when he scored eight times. Johnny transferred to Aldershot in September 1947 and then finally to Crystal Palace in July 1949. When he retired he had made 58 Football League appearances, scoring six goals.

Sherwood subsequently set up refreshment stalls in Elm Park and lived in Reading for the rest of his life, working as a bookie and a racing tipster. Johnny died in October 1985.

L.G, Stone

L.G. Stone, the Woking player, travelled with the Islington Corinthians only as far as Port Said where he was obliged to return to England through illness.

R.P. Tarrant

Dick Tarrant was the joker in the pack whilst on tour and had a hand in most of the mischief that was going on. Dick was an Irishman, who upon being released by Millwall joined Sutton United early in the 1932/33 season, at a time when the Surrey club was struggling. Tarrant found his form during the 1933/34 season, scoring 31 league and cup goals, and helped United to win the Surrey Senior Charity Shield for the first time and to reach the F.A. Amateur Cup quarter finals a year later.

In 1934/35 season, Tarrant became the first Sutton United player to gain international honours when he represented Ireland against England in an amateur international that year. He was to win further international caps against Scotland and Wales, and representative honours in games for Surrey and the Athenian League. Dick was a dashing centre forward who worked as a railway clerk.

William (Bill) Whittaker

Bill was an excellent centre-half who played the typical third back English game, prominent at the time. He was highly regarded and the '*Surrey Comet*' was moved to say '*Whittaker, of course is among the three best pivots in the amateur game,*'s which is why he earned the nickname 'Rock of Gibraltar.' Whittaker was to gain many honours, representing the Surrey F.A., the London F.A. and the A.F.A., but the highest one of all would come after his return from the world tour when he gained his only England amateur international cap in 1938/39 in a 5-2 victory over Wales at Cheltenham.

Whittaker began the 1937/38 season with Kingstonian, but his place was eventually taken by his brother. Bill did feature, however, in an impressive 8-0 victory over Oxford City, but the team struggled to build on this thereafter. Bill was also a talented cricketer and played for Surrey County Cricket Club's second eleven.

Ted Wingfield

Ted Wingfield at 5'11" was the more experienced of the two goal keepers selected for the tour and played for Romford who had just won the Athenian League for the second successive year with a truly amazing record. Of the 26 games played, Romford were to win all but two (one draw and one defeat).

Wingfield had gained an assortment of honours, representing the Football Association on six occasions, holding a county cap, and also appearing for the Southern Counties versus the Northern Counties. He had gained further honours and represented the

London League and took part in the international trial match in 1936.

Ted was 27 years old at the start of the tour and worked for a Bristol daily newspaper in their advertising department.

J.K. Wright

J.K. Wright was born in 1910, the son of the secretary of York City F.C. He began playing his football at Archbishop Holgate's Grammar School and furthered his education at St. Luke's, Exeter University. After leaving University he played for Nether Edge Amateurs and then Yorkshire Amateurs, before gaining employment as a school master at a school in Mitcham. It was at this point that he joined Wimbledon and appeared in their 1934/35 F.A. Amateur Cup final defeat to Bishop Auckland. Two years later, following his transfer to Dulwich Hamlet, Wright was to lift the cup with his new club who defeated Leyton 2-0.

Wright gained many honours and represented Sheffield and Hallamshire (Northern Counties Amateur Champions in 1931) on five occasions, 1933,'34,'35,'36,'37 and had represented Surrey eight times. He took part in the following International Trials: Northern Counties v Southern Counties in 1932, Southern Counties v Northern Counties in 1935, and represented the London F.A. versus Diables Rouges (Belgium), London University and Birmingham.

CHAPTER FOUR

FLOODLIGHTS AND KINGS

Tom Smith had completed the arrangements as far as humanly possible and selected a team that was capable of upholding the honour of the club and British football in general. The time had now come for the tourists to depart. Clark recounted his feelings:

'Kicking a Football Around the World, How romantic that sounds, how brimful of potential mystery and adventure, how thrilling and exciting, the breath-taking anticipation of new places, new people, new experiences. Yes, there is no doubt the prospect was encompassed by all these factors for the nineteen young men, plus coach and manager who set out on October 4th, 1937, to explore the world with a football – certainly a voyage into the unknown. Anticipation is one thing, however, and more often than not the actuality proves to be a fish of a different species. What secrets did it uncover, what thrills did it provide, what celebrities did it introduce to this wandering tribe of sportsmen?' [1]

It was the evening of Monday 4th October 1937 and the tour party had gathered at the station with family, friends and photographers ready to wave them off. A mixture of excitement and apprehension gripped the tourists as Clark continues:

'I had the good fortune to be selected the captain of Islington Corinthians, and when I sat down, having packed my smaller cabin baggage on the evening of October 3rd, my reflections, if not philosophic, were certainly not shallow. This was a big thing, a grim adventure carrying quite a deal of responsibility for a young man of 26.....

...but when the train moved out a very quiet, subdued and reflective atmosphere prevailed amongst the travelling party.

This was it. After months of anticipation the day had at last come; to bring what? Nobody knew. If our success on the first leg in Europe was, to put it mildly, limited, then nobody knew that we might never leave Europe at all. And that after practically half the team had thrown in jobs at home. We simply had to succeed in our continental matches if we were to fulfil our booking for Egypt on the 'Esperia' at Genoa (sic).'[2]

The first destination was Holland, a late change to the original itinerary, and they arrived safely the following day in the port of Rotterdam. The club was no stranger to Holland, although it was for some players the first adventure. The modern image of Holland is either related to drugs and sex or what the tourist board wishes to promote - an artificial amalgam of tulips, windmills, clogs and Edam cheese. It was, however, a fast developing industrial country in the 1930's and suffered severely during the Depression with hundreds of thousands of unemployed workers struggling to survive. Following the great creative period of the late 19th century, the country had entered a period of intellectual sterility, marked by stabilisation and organisation. The historian Pieter Geyl paints a bleak and worrying picture:

'When I went back to Holland at the beginning of 1936 after my twenty-two years' residence in London, I found a tense political situation prevailing there. There was the great depression, attended by unemployment, against which the Conservative Government, thinking of nothing but economizing and balancing the budget, stood helpless. And there was, just across the frontier, the frightening spectacle of German National-Socialist dynamism.'[3]

With this dark cloud hanging over the country the Islington Corinthians commenced their first game of what was to become an epic world tour in The Hague on 5th October 1937. The Islington Corinthians being full of enthusiasm for the first game faced VUC under floodlights, a novel experience for the players involved. It took the tourists time to adjust to these different conditions and although they enjoyed 70% of the play, they could not find a way past their opponents' goal-keeper, a man mountain of 6'4'' who gave a remarkable display and who had been tipped as a future Dutch international. Clark was later quoted: – *'He did not think much of the game under artificial light with a white ball. Some players could not adapt to the conditions.'*[4]

The tourists progressed to Amsterdam (a city whose population in 1938 was 793,000), where they would face Haarlem, the only undefeated club in Holland at the time and the reigning Dutch champions. Johnny Sherwood opened the I.C.'s goal account on the trip as the tourists won their first game 2-0. Their third game in three days resulted in a 1-1 draw with Amsterdam DWV. This match brought the Dutch leg of the trip to a conclusion, and Tom Smith recounted: *'the Dutch were good footballers, but they lacked that 'direct thrust' as witnessed in English soccer.'*[5]

The Islington Corinthians left Amsterdam on the 9th October 1937, destined for Switzerland, and arrived later that day in Zurich. Switzerland, which had established its neutrality at the 1815 Council of Vienna, was a popular destination for the touring British sides in the 1930's. It was a time when national identity was in question under the threat from neighbouring Nazi Germany, and is characterised by what was called

'Spiritual Defence.' It was ultimately the only predominantly German speaking country where the media actually opposed the Nazis, but as the subsequent scandal over stolen Jewish treasures reveals, it was still very much dependant economically on its neighbours.

Details of the Swiss part of the tour have been difficult to trace, but in Zurich Winterthur were defeated 3-0. Two days later (12th October 1937), the tourists defeated Berne 4-1 under floodlights. The European stage of the tour had been a success; this was essential if the rest of the trip was to take place. Smith spoke proudly of the team's record:

'On the continent, the team was not a very great attraction, Mr. Smith related, because many good English teams had previously visited such countries as Holland and Switzerland. 'But,' he added, 'this is the first time an English amateur side has been through the Continent without being defeated, and that is quite an encouraging start.'[6]

The Islington Corinthians continued their voyage south through Italy to Naples, stopping only to visit the ruins of Pompeii. The players enjoyed a well earned break from football at this point and Clark waxed lyrical:

'Now we were into the old 'med' – that haven of azure blue skies and still, limpid waters. A quick tour of Naples, Vesuvius and Pompeii. All the time it was sunshine, new things, new adventure. Yes, the 'Med.' It was all right until we passed Scylla and Charybdis and thence out into the Black unknown. How I remember the first slight movement of that old barge – it was almost imperceptible at first but soon it gained momentum and joined harmony with the overpowering rhythm of the wind and sea.

Things were now somewhat unsettling and quite a few anxious glances were exchanged amongst the boys assembled in the tourist saloon for the usual sing-song. Bill Whittaker had put away his ukulele with what he thought was deliberate intent. But some of us were not to be foxed. Harry Lowe – ex-Spurs and our trainer – casually asked me if I had paid a visit to the ship's billiards saloon and on my affirmation reply asked poor Johnny Sherwood if he'd like a game of snooker. 'Yes,' said Johnny, 'anything to get away from this.' And then he looked around and saw the smirks on the faces of those still retaining a little control. 'You rats,' he expostulated, and dived for the side – and that was that.'[7]

Next the I.C.'s journeyed to the country of the Sphinx and Pyramids, an ancient land which had long caught the imagination of the British public. At this point Egypt enjoyed a hollow independence, with Britain having close political links to the country. Egypt had been granted independence by Great Britain in 1922, when the Mohammed Ali dynasty was effectively returned to power. The British, however, maintained their influence in the region because the King did not enjoy the popular support of his people and so was reliant on British troops to maintain his authority. The popular

Above: Islington Corinthians arrival in Alexandria

support he was lacking gravitated towards the Wafd Party, who completed a power triangle which hamstrung Egyptian politics during the 1920's and 1930's. Each group helped keep the other groups in check; for instance, periodic agitation by the Wafd Party against continuing British influence would be countered by the King exercising his right to dissolve parliament.

This uneasy arrangement had continued up to 1936 when Britain and Egypt signed the Anglo-Egyptian Treaty. This was a result of Egyptian fears of an Italian invasion (Tripolitania having been annexed in 1912 and Abysinnia as recently as May 1936). The treaty limited British troops in Egypt to the protection of the Suez Canal and defence in case of war, but it effectively ensured that Great Britain held the upper hand in coming years.

The voyage on the 'Esperia' from Naples to Alexandria, was not quite as relaxing as probably hoped, as a storm raged during the sea crossing until they reached their destination. In fact it was some of the roughest weather that the Mediterranean was capable of producing, and the tourists had to survive on just an orange juice diet for the duration of the voyage. All the party were relieved to reach land on 20th October 1937. Clark recorded their arrival:

Left: A.J. Martin 'I must get out of this suit and into some tropical gear'

'Arrival at Alex probably created the most lasting of all our many and varied experiences throughout the trip. When still about an hour out from port we were pleasantly surprised by the approach of a very exclusive launch carrying dignitaries representing all branches of Egyptian sport. Garlands of flowers – how we eventually learned to abhor these, for we had them all the way to Hawaii – were deposited round our necks, photographs taken, and salaams freely and generously exchanged. Once in port it was interesting to contrast the phlegmatic British Raj, patiently awaiting the arrival of his travelling friends, with the excitement, shouting, and animal-like intensity of the Egyptian mob, held back by police carrying scout poles.'[8]

The launch party included a host of local dignitaries; Fahmy Wissa Bey (president) and Negib Awny (Secretary) representing the Egyptian .F.A.; Mr C.F. Beyts and Mr. C. Davey representing the British Legion; Bimbashi Luxor, Mr. H. Wolf of the Egyptian Gazette and many others. They were then taken sightseeing around the city (including a visit to the Alexandria stadium).

Alexandria was a curious oasis in Africa, with its Mediterranean style of life described by author Raymond Flower as follows:

'Day to day business may have been conducted in a miasma of chicanery, always hovering on the edge of sharp practise, but the social scene was infinitely cosmopolitan with a seductive blend of leisure and lushness which echoed but

51

assuaged the international radiance of Rome, the scruffy patricianship of Athens, and the parochial' dolce-vita' of Palermo or Algiers.'[9]

Flower continued to say that it was normal to dine out as frequently as four or five nights a week, with a minimum of 16 people expected at a table. The women in society would not dream of wearing the same dress out twice!

The I.C.'s could not stay long, (although they would return) and caught the afternoon express to Cairo, arriving there at 7.25 p.m and receiving another warm reception at the station. The welcoming committee consisted of members of the Cairo FA and a number of local players. After large bouquets were exchanged the players were taken to the National Hotel. The party were impressed with their reception and Smith, who would become the main spokesman, stated:

'We are very touched at this warm-hearted reception,' said Mr. T. Smith, the honorary secretary of the Club and the manager and organizer of the present tour, to an Egyptian Gazette representative last night. 'We never expected anything like this and we are very grateful to all concerned.'[10]

Smith continued to say he felt the side was blending well; the defence was becoming a strong unit, whilst the attack was coming together. Smith's plans would be thrown in to turmoil, however, as his squad was hit by a bout of food poisoning, which he later recounted to the Islington Rotary Club on his return:

'He commenced by speaking of the manner in which he had to doctor members of the team who were taken ill with 'gyppy tummy' whilst playing in Egypt. Of the 19 members of the party six were taken ill and one had to return home. Financial considerations prevented the calling in of doctors except in cases of high temperature, and Rot. Smith described how he diagnosed the players' complaints and acted as nurse to them as well. The result of his homely administrations was that all the boys recovered and were quite fit by the time they reached India.'[11]

This sickness was probably not surprising when you take into account Clark's less than enthusiastic description of Cairo (a city,even then, of over one million inhabitants):

'There was a Maleesh from our taxi-driver after he had smashed beyond repair an almost new Studebaker and nearly sent us to kingdom come in the process by his awful driving; Gyppy Tummy and Dengue, beggars exploiting crippled children – no poppa, no momma, no chow, no whiskey; pedlars and bootbacks; shopping touts and others; fly swatters and the sweetest, sickliest cakes in existence; camels and guides, and the whole juxtaposition of filth, stench, dust and disease alongside the opulence and high living of the hotels and clubs.'[12]

On the day following their arrival in Cairo, the tourists enjoyed afternoon tea at the Agricultural Society Centre in Gezira and generally took things easy. This was a

Above: The King Farouk Stadium

timely break, for next day the players faced tough opposition in the form of a Cairo XI at the Prince Farouk Stadium. The Egyptians had spent the weeks preceding the I.C's arrival preparing their team and had recorded some impressive victories over the British army. The Egyptians were excited by the tourists' visit and were determined to make a good impression.

The tourists were leaving nothing to chance and had brought along their mascot which the Egyptian Gazette described as *'a benevolent looking lion, gazing tipsily at the play from the cinder track.'*[13] There was a slight drizzle at kick-off time, which must have made the tourists feel more at home when the match commenced. The game itself was dominated by the defences of both sides and honours finished even. Pat Clark contained the local star Mustapha Latif despite picking up an injury after 27 minutes. No score occurred until five minutes before the interval when Cairo took the lead following sloppy play by the I.C.'s, Manning having miss-kicked his attempted clearance. It was to remain this way until the 75th minute when J. Miller scored direct from a corner (or a flag kick as the *'Egyptian Gazette'* described it). The Islington Corinthians might even have snatched victory as Tarrant hit the post late on, and Wright saw a tremendous shot tipped away by the Egyptian goalkeeper.

For the next match Islington Corinthians returned to Alexandria (the second town of Egypt with a population in excess of 500,000), where they were introduced as the

Left: King Farouk of Egypt watching the match between Islington Corinthians and Alexandria.

famous Scottish side! This much remarked comment caused great amusement among the tourists and was corrected in the *'Egyptian Gazette'*:

*'The visitors, contrary to advertisements and handbills distributed in Alexandria throughout the week, are not 'The famous Scottish team' nor 'The best Amateur team in the world' but just a London Club, reinforced by members of other London club sides, with no pretensions to being anything more than Saturday afternoon amateurs, making a tour of the world and playing the game for the game's sake.'*14

The match took place at the Municipal Stadium, where there was a good attendance of some 5,000 spectators. This surprised the writers of the *'Egyptian Gazette'* as public interest in local league matches had fallen recently to an all-time low.

One interested spectator was King Farouk, along with several of his ministers and high officials. King Farouk, or to give him his full title; 'His Majesty Farouk I, by the grace of God, King of Egypt and of Sudan, Sovereign of Nubia, of Kordofan and of Darfur,' was no stranger to the game having been educated at the Royal Military Academy in Woolwich. Farouk had been crowned the previous year at the tender age of 16, and he later managed to keep Egypt out of the Second World War. In 1952, following the Egyptian Revolution, he was forced to abdicate and spent the rest of his life in exile in Italy. It has been rumoured that the actor David Suchet modelled his moustache for detective Hercule Poirot on King Farouk's distinctive adornment.

The I.C.'s began the match with the sun at their backs, and were to produce what the locals conceded was a competent exhibition of defensive football. If the attack had been anywhere close to the standard of the rear-guard, they would have won with goals to spare. This criticism was not entirely fair (in fact Smith had half his team ill in bed), but in the early stages of the tour the defence was certainly the stronger department of the team.

The Alexandria team was not completely without blame for negativity as Tarrant was completely shut out of the game and Read, who did some good work on the right wing, was confronted with some unorthodox tackling. The I.C.'s took the lead on 28 minutes when a corner from Pearce was cleared only to Read, who passed to Bradbury who shot at goal. The ball was headed clear to Sherwood, who drove the ball home from 25 yards.

The game swung more in favour of the I.C.'s when Johnny Miller replaced Pearce on the left wing at half-time, and he began to open up the Alexandria defence. Alexandria equalised during the second half, but this just spurred the tourists on and they did not put a foot wrong for the rest of the game as Johnny Miller controlled the proceedings. With 15 minutes remaining Miller and Sherwood combined with a bout of passing between each other and the former eventually scored with a glorious shot from the edge of the penalty area. The first victory in Egypt had been achieved and on the conclusion of the match the players lined up in front of the Royal enclosure, gave three resounding cheers for the King and were then each presented to His Majesty. After the game the King hosted a dinner in the tourists' honour.

Islington Corinthians were given four days rest following this match, and on their return to Cairo they visited the Pyramids which were situated about five miles from the edge of the city. The tourists were taken by car along a wide modern hard-surfaced highway, which impressed them despite the snack counters which lined it until the edge of the desert. They were then shocked on visiting the Kit-Kat (Cairo's famous nightclub), when it was found that the price of the Champagne was 30 shillings a bottle!

On 29th October 1937 the team faced a rematch with the Cairo XI, this time at the C.I.S.C. ground at Zamalek. The Egyptian selectors were intent on improving on the previous result and made three alterations to the attack. Among the players dropped was the local star Mohamed Latif, who was described as one of the finest Egyptian players ever, having recently been playing for Glasgow Rangers. The team was changed further when three new defensive players were introduced in an effort to contain Sherwood and Tarrant.

Islington Corinthians again saved their best for the second half after going in at the interval one goal behind, albeit against the run of play. Equality was restored on 56 minutes, when Read shot past Yehia. The I.C.'s quickly gained the advantage after this when Tarrant's shot was punched away by Yehia, but only as far as W. Miller who

Left: Rent a camel

Left: The Sphinx

Right: The Pyramids

scored from the rebound. The I.C.'s performance did not impress the *'Egyptian Gazette'* who described it merely as robust and efficient, due to better stamina.

The team travelled next to Port Said in what was called the Canal Zone, (the strip of territory where British troops protecting the Suez Canal were based). It had been hoped that a game with the United Services would be arranged on the Slade Ground to enable the troops to see them, and although this unfortunately did not materialize, the match played represented the next best thing.

The tourists were to face a Canal Zone XI at the Port Fouad Stadium against a side which contained four members of last season's champions, (Egyptian Athletic) and five members of the current championship leaders. The Egyptians had abandoned their old method of sharing selected players throughout the clubs and were confident that the local players could do well against the tourists. Their hopes would prove to be well founded.

Admission was set at P.T. 22 (100 piastres made up one Egyptian pound worth just over £1 Sterling) for reserved seating, P.T. 11 and P.T. 5 ½ including tax and this helped to attract 3,000 to the match. It was a game of missed chances by the Islington Corinthians and they went behind on 29 minutes when Uva scored after Longman had parried a shot from Sophoulis. Seven minutes later the I.C.'s equalised when Read set up Bradbury and the inside-right took full advantage.

The I.C.'s were hampered by injuries, however, as Clark was hurt early in the game and this eventually led to their downfall. Within three minutes of the I.C.'s equaliser, the Canal Zone restored their advantage when Uva scored again, and the home side added a third goal two minutes after half time. It got even worse when Sophoulis beat three men and Manakli scored from his centre. W. Miller and Manning were then injured, the latter player being of little use when he returned to the field (his injury would keep him out of the side for three weeks). These mishaps compounded the tourists' problems and on 62 minutes Uva completed his hat-trick. The I.C.'s had no answer to this (particularly as they then had only eight fit men) and the final score was a 1-4 defeat.

The inevitable post match inquest led to Smith to comment:

'the touring team's manager said that he ought to have replaced Manning (right-back) and Miller (left out-side), who were both hurt in the second half but he is not in favour of the substitute system and does not like bringing on reserves unless a player is incapable of taking any further part in the game.'[15]

Overall the local press was divided in its opinion of the Islington Corinthians, as this comment in The Egyptian shows:

'The surprising feature of the tour has been the many adverse comments that have appeared regarding these games in many newspapers, the most unjustified coming from a Sunday weekly appearing in French.

....The main objections to the tourists were firstly, that they did not play sufficiently well to completely annihilate the locals, and that it would have been better to have brought out some Central European professional team to do so – as then our local footballers would have been able to progress through playing against class footballers. Secondly, that they were not the Corinthians at all, while the Sunday paper we alluded to went so far as to allege that they pretended to be the original Corinthians, and inferred that the Egyptian Football Association had been misled in accepting their propositions in Egypt.' [16]

The *'Egyptian Gazette'* went on to comment that this was unjustified, and that following the Austrian side Admira's visit, local football had suffered. It was felt that only through good behaviour and whole-hearted training could football in Egypt progress. It firmly put down the accusation about the I.C.'s claiming to be the real Corinthians, and explained both that the club was only five years old and that the reason for the tour originated in an invitation from the Chinese. It concluded by commenting that the I.C.'s were an excellent bunch of sportsmen, which at least shows that they had made an impression. Unfortunately at this point L. Stone was obliged to return to England due to illness, and Smith had even fewer options for the daunting tour ahead of him and the team.

The post match entertainment took the form of a late tea at the Casino Palace Hotel, in the presence of the Governor, the Commandant of Police, the British Vice-Consul, officials from the Egyptian F.A. (from both Cairo and Port Said), presidents of the local clubs and some press representatives. After the tea Mohamed Eff. Moussa, secretary of the Egyptian Athletic Club and of the local federation, made the following speech.

'On behalf of the Egyptian Football Association in the Canal Zone I have the greatest pleasure in welcoming you, from the bottom of my heart.

Although this is the first time an English Amateur team has visited Egypt, I think I should mention that the credit for the progress of association football in Egypt goes to the English, as they were the first to plant the seeds of football in our sporting fields. We are now reaping the sweet fruits of their planting and on this particular occasion I am proud to express our sincere thanks for all they have done for us in this respect.

If I may be permitted to say that the political Treaty which was recently ratified between Egypt and Great Britain, has stabilized the relations between the two countries on a sound basis, I have no hesitation in declaring now that your visit to our country has not only strengthened the bonds of the sporting spirit, but will also do much to cement the foundations of the friendship between our two nations (Applause).

In fact as football has so widely been spread to all parts of the globe and become for millions of people the most attractive game of the day, a word of praise should be given to England, the teachers, who are principally responsible for football reaching the position it holds today.

While thanking you for the sportsmanlike manner in which you played I must also thank our Higher Committee in Cairo for giving us the unique opportunity of watching such a wonderful team as yours and no doubt your visit to Egypt has been highly successful both to players and to the numerous spectators who were very delighted to see your remarkable and magnificent play. Although you were beaten I am sure everyone will agree with me that you were by no means disgraced.

In brief I repeat my thanks and congratulations and assure you again that your visit will leave a deep and lasting remembrance in our hearts and minds.

I sincerely trust that you have enjoyed yourselves during your short stay in our country and as this is your last match in Egypt, I take the opportunity of wishing you on behalf of all sportsmen in general, and all Egyptians in particular, a very happy and pleasant voyage, the best of luck in all your forthcoming matches and at last a safe return to your homes.' (applause)[17]

Tom Smith replied to this in his usual diplomatic manner:
'(Smith) said how much pleasure it had given them to play in Port Said. Referring to the previous speech, he said he did think sport does cement friendship between nations. 'Looking round now,' said Mr. Smith, 'I can see our boys have got together with yours at the various tables and quickly become friends. Today we were beaten, admittedly by a better side, but we are coming back shortly to alter that. On arriving in Egypt we were told Cairo was the best team in the country, beg to differ, we have met the best team to-day, and when we do return we shall play Port Said first...

In concluding I must say we like Egypt and we like the people. I mentioned about our return here. It is not the waters of the Nile which will call us back, but the wonderful hospitality of your people. (applause)'[18]

The I.C.'s were indeed becoming perfect ambassadors for Britain and had the social skills to make new friends everywhere they went. All that was left was for P.B. Clark, the visitors' captain, to present a banner to the Port Said skipper, Helmi, as a memento of the match.

The tourists returned with many amusing anecdotes and Smith later recounted this story about the weather in Egypt:

'He told an amusing story of how the Cairo weather prophets proved to be wrong, 'They told us,' he said, 'that they knew exactly what the weather would be like during our stay in Egypt, and that we should have no rain as it was the dry season. Well, it so

Above: The 'Conte Rosso' which was torpedoed and sunk by the British in 1941 with the loss of over 800 lives.

turned out that there was the worst rain-storm for years and the town was flooded out.'[19]

It was time for the tourists to depart for India. They sailed on the 'Conte Rosso' (the Red Count) down the Suez Canal into the Red Sea, passing East Africa, Saudi Arabia, Yeman and Oman and on to Bombay, (now known as Mumbai). The tourists were constantly amazed at the sights that confronted them and during the voyage Smith recalled:

'...the boat called in at an Italian East African port and they had their first sight of Abyssinians, wiry little men working on the quay-side and carrying loads that looked far too heavy for them.'[20]

The team was soon to reach India.

CHAPTER FIVE

PERISCOPES AND DAGGERS

The Islington Corinthians arrived in India on 11th November 1937. The British Raj as India was known was an enormous country and in 1937 included the areas which make up modern day Pakistan and Bangladesh (and until April that year, Burma). King Emperor George VI was the head of state and his representative there was the Marquess of Linlithgow as Viceroy and Governor-general of India. India in reality was governed by an authoritarian administration in London where the cabinet included the Marquess of Zetland as Secretary of State for India. Power was maintained through the police, of which there were 200,000 during the 1930's, the majority of whom were under the control of British officers.

Tensions had risen, particularly since World War One, with a growing clamour for independence by the Indian people. The Indian National Congress of 1885 had first adopted the policy and, led by Gandhi and Nehru, it had since developed into a campaign of civil disobedience. At the time of the Islington Corinthians' visit the Muslim League was also emerging as the voice of Islam and in 1940 this organisation was to call for the partition of India along religious lines.

The I.C.'s visit coincided with a quieter period in the pursuit of independence, but with British economic interests declining it ultimately proved successful and India and Pakistan became independent countries in 1947. Later, in 1971, East Pakistan was to gain independence (as Bangladesh) from West Pakistan following a nine month war, in which Bangladesh was supported militarily by India.

As the liner 'Conte Rosso' approached Bombay, the team was met on board by Mr A.C. Hinrichs, President of the Western India FA, Mr E.J. Turner the Honorary Secretary of the Association and members of the WIFA committee. Mr Hinrichs also delivered messages of welcome which he handed to Tom Smith.

With the team firmly on dry land it was time for the official welcome. The Viceroy of India said: *'As Patron-in-Chief of the All-India Football Federation I welcome to India*

61

the Islington Corinthians football team and wish them a successful Tour.[1] These comments were reiterated by Sir Roger Lumley who was Governor of Bombay: *'As Patron of Western India Football Association, I bid you and your team welcome to Bombay, and express the hope that you will have a very enjoyable and successful tour throughout India.'*[2]

Tom Smith then answered questions from the local press and the interview is recorded here:

(Tom Smith) *'Told of the fact that his side would meet bare-footed players for the first time, in Calcutta, and that they would probably find the pace faster than they expected, Mr. Smith replied:- 'I do not think we need worry about that. If my men can settle down to the conditions underfoot, I feel confident they will deal with the pace.'*

Mr. Smith remarked that his side were eager to get into action again for they had had little or no exercise aboard. The side were looking forward to playing at Calcutta and Rangoon, particularly the latter port, for, as Mr. Smith put it, 'I have heard a good deal of Rangoon football, and would like to see my men win over there.'[3]

The team were then taken on a sightseeing tour of Bombay and it is interesting at this point to look at Pat Clark's recollections:

'Our reception in Bombay was, if anything, more colourful than that of Alex. The Indians on board had given us just an inkling of what was coming, for nearing port all European dress was discarded to be replaced by the blues, greens, yellows, mauves, violets, helios, of the turbans and saris. But soon we had to tear ourselves away from the ship's rail to lend an attentive ear to a speech of welcome from the West Indian F.A.

It brought our first encounter with Percy Gupta, that man of action and indefatigable energy, with the deep black eyes which flashed when he was crossed but which laughed with uncontrolled abandon when amused. I should think that Percy has travelled farther and under more varied capacities than any other sportsman in the world. He took the Indian hockey team to the Olympic Games at Berlin in 1936, the football team to the Far East and Australia on several occasions, the Indian cricket team to Britain in 1946, another team, I know not what, to Los Angeles in 1932, and now he hopes to come to London as general manager of all Indian sportsmen participating in the Olympic Games in 1948.

And Jimmy James, his assistant manager, What a life that young man was going to lead in the next eight weeks. It would have been kinder to let him know in advance. Jimmy, an Anglo-Indian, had two solitary tusks in front and the rest a gaping void. How he liked to assert his authority on the six bearers who were with us throughout the Indian part of the tour. They were at our beck and call every minute of every hour of every day for eight weeks. Old David, 70 if a day, who proudly told me of his

Christian leanings and of the famous Sahibs – some imaginary, I'm afraid – to whom he had given faithful service in the past. Abdul was another such who nearly broke poor Jimmy's heart for he was always on the scrounge, making his own little crust out of every transaction.

Plied with most luxurious landaus and limousines, we were immediately whisked off to the Taj Mahal Hotel for breakfast and so on to a sight-seeing tour of the city. We stopped at the colossal markets in the centre of Bombay. In the course of our tour a most likeable Parsee host told us all about the Towers of Silence and the vultures which swooped down on the corpses laid bare to their depredations over iron gates.

By this time the boys had become aware of the utter apprehension and foreboding which one of the party, Peter by name, regarded all new oriental experience. Dick Tarrant going through the market picked up an old joint which had been well stripped, wrapped it in paper. Peter was manoeuvred into the front seat of a large tourer and four or five boys, including Dick, were piled in behind. The Parsee had been well primed by Dick to back up the act which was about to take place.

As we were climbing an incline not far from the Towers, with the necessary swooping and squawking of vultures creating the right atmosphere, Dick suddenly let out a howl of horror in which the others readily joined. He held the joint under Peter's nose and asked the Parsee to explain where it had come from. He immediately played up by casually explaining that this sort of thing happened every day. It was the arm, but no, the leg, of some corpse laid up there to rest in the Towers and dropped by one of the raiding vultures. There was really nothing to it. Poor Peter. First he went pale and then politely asked the Parsee to stop the car as he didn't feel well. It was the first of many cruel practical jokes, but sometimes I consoled myself by the hope that most times Peter had his tongue in his cheek.

*Unfortunately there was no game in Bombay. The Indian F.A. having shied at the financial obligations involved in our visit had leased the responsibility to private enterprise. Mr. Hedwards, the promoter, put up the £2,000 necessary and demanded certain tithes from every district visited. Bombay couldn't guarantee the necessary amount and so they could have no game. But that didn't prevent the W.I.F.A. extending hospitality which was superseded nowhere in India.'*4

At the lunch at the Taj Mahal Hotel, Mr. Hinrichs toasted 'His Majesty the King' and 'Our Guests' and went on to say that he was glad the boat had been late as it had given him more time to prepare the welcome. Hinrichs continued by talking about the problems he had experienced in arranging games in Bombay:

'He stated that he had discussed with Mr. Tom Smith, the present situation which prevented the visitors from playing a game in Bombay. The inability to arrange a match for them in Bombay was no fault of the W.I.F.A., for the proposition put forward to them by those who controlled the arrangements was an impossible one. The W.I.F.A.

in return had made a sporting offer, but unfortunately the Indian Football Federation, did not accept it.

Bombay, Mr. Hinrichs added, was not as fortunate as Calcutta in being able to see the visitors in action, but he stated it was chiefly due to the fact that Bombay was not as keen on soccer as Calcutta was.'5

Smith replied in his address:

'Talking of the forthcoming match against the Mohammedan Sporting at Calcutta, Mr. Smith stated he had heard quite an amount regarding the Indians' play, nothing, however, to their discredit. He was looking forward to that match in Calcutta, and added that if the Mohammedan Sporting beat his side he would go back and tell the English soccer authorities that he needed a far stronger side next time he undertook a trip to India.

Before concluding, he stated he had great confidence in his players. They had pulled the game out of the fire on several occasions on the Continent, and he was sure they could do it in India, if called upon. He assured the gathering that he was not unduly over-confident but stated that if beaten in India, as they may perhaps be, his side would take defeat in a sporting manner.'6

The I.C.'s tight schedule meant that they barely had time to stretch their legs in a 'kickabout' on the Cooperage before leaving for Calcutta; (the delay in arriving in India meant that the team would only reach their destination on the day of the first match). The journey itself across the breadth of India from Bombay to Calcutta in Bengal certainly opened a few eyes amongst the tourists as Smith later recalled:

'The train journey took two days and nights, and in the course of it they were plagued by insects through leaving the carriage windows open whilst passing through a swamp and were everywhere garlanded by enthusiastic native students.'7

Clark was somewhat more colourful in his account of the journey:

'Two and a half days of weary travel brought us across India, and anxious days they were for Percy Gupta. A lot of our feeding had to be done in railway canteens en route and, needless to say, departure times were very often late. The boys simply refused to budge until they had their fill, whilst in the meantime Percy would be running backwards and forwards, bribing first the driver and then the guard not to leave without us.'8

Clark continued:

'We were down to play against India's champion side, Mohammedan Sporting, a couple of hours after arrival in Calcutta. About five o'clock in the morning of the day we were due to arrive at Howrah Station, Calcutta, the first of our receptions began.

64

Above: Islington Corinthians' arrival in Calcutta

Our two coaches were suddenly invaded at some station in the back of beyond by a flood of dark skinned beaming faces, the wearers of whom were bearing mounds of garlands and sheets of paper bearing speeches of welcome. Our first reaction was 'thank goodness that's over; we should be in Calcutta soon.' But on enquiry from Percy we learned that the train wasn't due in Calcutta until two in the afternoon – and that the same reception programme was forthcoming at every stopping station for the next four hundred miles. The mounds of flowers piled up so fast that certain members suggested launching out in the florist trade. Two o'clock eventually arrived to a scene on Howrah which really had to be seen to be believed. The Indian Press expressed itself thus in the midst of half-page photographs and inch-high headlines of welcome.'[9]

The tour party arrived in Calcutta on the Bengal Nagpur Railway Mail Train on the 13th November 1937, and again experienced an impressive reception. The I.C.'s were keenly anticipated visitors to the former capital and the two leading clubs, Mohan Bagun and Mohammedan Sporting Club, had been hard at work practising for the forthcoming matches. The Islington Corinthians were destined to enjoy their time in Calcutta and were taken to the film studios in Calcutta, before going out with some of the actresses. It was during their stay here that they managed to catch up for quiet drinks with Bill Edrich, Norman Yardley, and Alf Gover who were part of Tennyson's 1937-38 cricket tour to India when five unofficial test matches were played.

Howrah Station, the scene of their arrival, was flooded by an enthusiastic crowd waiting to get a glimpse of the foreign football stars. As the train steamed into the station, there was a big surge towards the compartment where the players were sitting. Once order was restored Mr. Gupta (Secretary of the Indian F.A.) introduced the tourists to the Maharaja of Santosh. The Maharaja then read out a long, highly emotional and somewhat wearisome address of which the main points were:

'It gives me very great pleasure to welcome to Calcutta the Islington Corinthians in the name of the sporting citizens of the second city of the British Empire which is still the greatest football confederacy in the East....

Our guests represent the amateur footballers of a great country which has thrilled our people through and through by its rigorous games and manly sports. Besides, they bring with them to this country a reputation which is magnetic to say the least of it.'[10]

Pat Clark summarised events at Howrah Station later:

'The anticipation of the soccer fans of Calcutta did at last crystalise when the I.C.'s reached Howrah on Saturday afternoon by the B.N.R. Bombay Mail. The admiration of the infatuated crowd found such a spontaneous expression as must not have failed to touch the hearts of the visitors. Through the hour of the day was inconvenient, Sporting Calcutta was well represented on the Howrah platform, and, long before the mail was due, the hero worshippers were seen to stream in bearing their floral offerings of various artistic design. Numerous ladies draped in charming sarees lent a touch of colour to the whole scene. As the train steamed in there was a concerted rush to locate the tourists, and as they were occupying coupes at the back of the train, very soon the whole crowd gravitated to that quarter. The Maharaja of Santosh led the welcoming party. Now followed the general garlanding ceremony when garlands were presented by the Maharaja of Santosh on behalf of the I.F.A., Knwaja Sir Nazim-ud-Dum (Sir Khwaja Nazim-ud-Din) *on behalf of the Mohammedan Community, by Mr. Gupta and Mr H. Edwards on behalf of the Organising Committee. The language was as flowery as the garlands.*

And so it was roses, roses all the way, with at least half a dozen biting, nasty little beasties on every petal.'[11]

Tom Smith, obviously exhausted after a long journey, thanked everyone with a short snappy speech and said how much they were looking forward to the games. The reception closed with a poem written and read by the famous Hindu poet Mr. S.C. Talukdar of East Bengal, dedicated to the Islington Corinthians.

After two days travelling by train and numerous welcoming offerings, the exhausted tourists literally had to step off the train and onto the football pitch to face Mohammedan Sporting Club, the league champions for the previous four years and Indian F.A. Shield holders. The excitement in Calcutta was reaching fever pitch and it

66

Left: Islington Corinthians with
Major Higgins at Jamshedpur

was reported that by 10a.m. some 3,000 supporters were already in the stadium, four hours before the I.C.'s were even due to arrive in Calcutta!

At kick-off there were 50,000 spectators present and the ensuing goal-less draw was something of an anticlimax. The local press felt that the I.C.'s were unaccustomed to the fast pace of the game but continued:

'When they settled down, however, particularly in the second half they played delightful football, except in the all-important matter of scoring goals, and it was the general opinion that if play had been continued for another ten minutes, the visitors would have won.'[12]

The Islington Corinthians certainly had the greater share of the play and it was J.W. Miller, who came closest to breaking the deadlock.

The Islington Corinthians did break their Indian scoring duck the following day when they visited Jamshedpur, nicknamed the Steel City, a short journey from Calcutta. Here the I.C.'s were to face the All Blues, who were a purely Anglo-Indian and domiciled European side. The tourists gave a wonderful display of football and ran out 5-2 winners after two goals apiece by Dick Tarrant and Sonny Avery, and a single by Jack Braithwaite. After the match the team were entertained to lunch, but as Clark recalled, it did not go exactly to plan:

'Again there was the Rotary reception in Jamshedpur, Bengal (sic), when, to accommodate the extra guests, an old hall, after long disuse, was tidied up for the occasion. Everything went well until some bright spark thought fit to freshen the smoke-laden atmosphere with some fresh air from the electric fan. No sooner was this done than there ensued a general scamper from the room, led by George Dance. Rotarians and their guests went through windows and doors as though pursued by fiends. Indeed, they were in a sense. During the months of disuse the fan had obligingly accommodated a gentle, law-abiding nest of hornets. They took a dim view of being so

Above: The coin-toss before Islington Corinthians v Mohon Bagun

disturbed. After the local fire brigade had duly fumigated the place the reception proceeded to a normal completion.'[13]

The following day the Islington Corinthians beat All Blues again 1-0, before travelling back to Calcutta. It is quite possible that one of the practical jokes later recalled in the press on the Canadian part of the tour occurred here:

'The gip of the trip was pulled in India, according to Lowe. Each member of the team received a mysterious phone call on this particular morning, advising him to put on his dress suit and appear at a certain hour at the leading newspaper office for an exclusive interview with picture. Secrecy was the key word.

At the appointed hour 17 players came face to face, dressed in fish and tails, at the paper shop. There was no interview, no picture....but a lot of red faces. The designer of that prank is still at large but most of the lads figure his initials are H.L. and his last name Lowe.'[14]

Above: Islington Corinthians and Mohon Bagan

The Islington Corinthians' next game was on 16th November 1937 and they faced another tough proposition in the form of Mohon Bagun (champions in 1939), another of Calcutta's leading clubs. 40,000 supporters witnessed this match, with many thousands being unable to gain admission. Prior to the game the following incident occurred:

'...the local Maharaja donated a hunting leopard to the local team because the visiting Britishers had a stuffed lion as a mascot. The native Indians, as a gesture of sportsmanship had their live and adult leopard meet the dead British lion before the game, and it was very embarrassing to the home office in London, Mr. Smith tells me, to see the dominion leopard rip the stuffed lion to shreds with a few swipes of the paw.'[15]

The game itself against the barefooted footballers of Mohon Bagan resulted in a victory for the tourists. The Times of India praised the local team for keeping the score down and they worked hard with the *'tenacity of terriers.'* The I.C.'s were struggling in front of goal and the forwards had still to click as a unit, although it did not take long for the I.C.'s to score the only goal of the match. On 15 minutes Mohon Bagan were caught on the break and allowed Tarrant to score the winner. The locals almost equalised two minutes later, but this was the closest that they came. The I.C.'s had plenty of opportunities to extend their lead, but could not add to their total and the game petered out into a dull affair.

Above: Islington Corinthians and All-India in Calcutta

Left: A.J. Martin and Samad, bootless
Captain of All-India in Calcutta

70

The Islington Corinthians' next game occurred the following day against an Indian F.A. XI, and was marred by poor refereeing. The Islington Corinthians certainly could feel aggrieved that they did not secure victory as they were leading until three minutes from the end. The I.C.'s had taken the lead after 47 minutes when Len Bradbury scored after a mistake by Jumma Khan. The Indians responded and forced Longman into making three crucial saves, then with three minutes remaining a penalty was awarded for hand-ball against Eddy Martin. Despite protests by the tourists who surrounded the referee, in the hope he would alter his decision, Jumma Khan made no mistake in equalising from the spot. In the dying moments a free kick by Pat Clark took a deflection and hit the Indians' post.

The referee had been giving bad decisions all afternoon as this description of an earlier penalty decision against the I.C.'s testifies:

'The kick was taken by Taylor, but the ball hit the post and came back into play. Then to the amazement of the crowd the referee signaled for a free-kick to be taken by the visitors. The referee later explained his action by stating that as soon as the kick was taken Rahamat had rushed an opponent. The general opinion was that many wrong decisions were given. It was a tribute to the visitors that they kept their tempers until the end and played clean and sporting football.'[16]

Another curiosity in a lot of the games the Islington Corinthians played is recounted by Clark:

'Invariably in these games....the Indians, out of respect for their visitors, would don obviously new boots and trot out impeccably attired in proper League fashion. Immediately we scored, plump they would settle themselves on the grass, tear off their boots and stockings and reveal elastic bandages guarding shins and ankles. When this happened we prepared ourselves for fireworks, for this meant business, and they set about it in no small fashion. Their ball control was superb, their speed in possession devastating. Their shooting was shy, however, though the defence astounded me with the bigness and accuracy of their kicking.'[17]

The post-match dinner provided an interesting insight into how the Islington Corinthians' visit was perceived in India, as Clark recalled:

'Perhaps our greatest contribution to Indian sport is expressed in the words of Sir Nazim-ud-Dum (sic), a Cabinet Minister in Congress, who said on the eve of the All-Indian game:

'I want to give the I.C's a friendly warning. To-morrow something is going to happen which we politicians have been trying to achieve for years. Hindus, Moslems, Anglo-Indians, Parsees, the Bangals and Bengalees, Indian and European, all the communities of India will be united for the first-time. All their one common object will

Left: Indian Rickshaws

be that our local All-India team will lower the colours of the I.C.'s. Whether we win or lose we hope to watch a first-class match.'[18]

After one of the post-match dinners held by the Islington Corinthians' hosts in Calcutta, Dick Manning had the following adventure:

'Dick Manning somehow managed to wander away to the other side of the City, in I know not whose company, in the glad rags which the occasion demanded. Tom, Harry Lowe and myself were just arranging to contact the police at about 4 a.m. when we heard quite a furore outside the hotel.

There was Dick surrounded by about fifty coolies all laughing their heads off at the spectacle of Dick between the shafts of the rickshaw, and the rickshaw wallah inside grinning through his toothless mouth. Dick apparently had demanded transportation to the Grand Hotel at least a dozen times and each time the wallah responded with 'Me know, me know – hotel very good place.' Every time Dick eventually found himself outside some house of ill repute, and so, his patience exhausted but his sense of humour fortunately still preserved, he had ordered the rickshaw wallah into the rickshaw and had driven him back to the Grand. Now at 4 a.m. he was trying to get a rupee out of his passenger for the ride, much to the amusement of hosts of coolies.'[19]

The I.C.'s now enjoyed two days rest, the first of which saw them entertained to luncheon by the President of the governing body of the Indian F.A. At this dinner the Maharaja of Santosh made another of his famous speeches and stated:

'the tourists were a well-balanced, well-built and magnificent lot. Their standard of physical fitness would furnish an object lesson to Indian players. He hoped the seeds of friendship sown would be enduring.'[20]

Above: Islington Corinthians with two Indian actresses visit the film studios in Calcutta

Tom Smith replied, saying that the I.C.'s had had a wonderful time so far in India and that he was struck by the hospitality of the people. He proceeded to make the Maharaja an honorary member of the Islington Corinthians, and in return the Indian F.A. presented badges to the tourists. The following day the team were guests at a tea party at the Grand Hotel hosted by their first opponents in India, the Mohammedan Sporting Club.

On 20th November 1937 the Islington Corinthians played against an All-India XI. This was their last game in Calcutta until Christmas when they returned at the end of the Indian leg of their tour. Clark gives the following account of the team's experiences on Calcutta match days, although he seems to have combined the experiences of several games into one:

'*As we drove to the Grand Hotel along Chowringee there came into view a sight I shall remember as long as I live. Temporary stands were erected on three sides of the playing pitch, but these were only barely visible, for the whole maidan, which appeared to be comparable to Hyde Park in area, was one mass of white linen. This was our crowd for the afternoon match. Various articles were carried by each and every spectator, which on closer inspection proved to be home-made periscopes, umbrellas and wads of newspaper. The latter appointments had us guessing, and it was not until our third match, when the All India XI scored the first goal against us in*

73

India, that we learned their purpose. The crowd simply went berserk, umbrellas were opened and shut with terrific rapidity and newspapers were torn into a million shreds.

The mad satanic roar of the adjacent crowd had no sooner died down than it was taken up by a more distant crowd who had just learned of the score, and the process was repeated on the far fringes of that terrific 100,000 crowd. The boys were utterly speechless in their reaction to this outburst, but, recovering quickly, settled down to business and scored two quick winning goals. At least fifteen minutes from the end of the game the long procession started leaving, exhibiting that mysterious fatalism which we encountered throughout the East. The self-same ceremony repeated itself wherever we got a couple of goals lead.' [21]

Tom Smith also described his experiences, probably of an earlier match:

'Seats had been erected to accommodate 30,000 spectators, whilst another 5,000, according to some local rule, were allowed to stand free at one end of the ground. I should think all of them had periscopes through which they watched the play. Every tree round the ground, and there were plenty of them, was black with natives and a large hill at the back which extended about half a mile was covered by natives who could have seen very little of the play. The enthusiasm was terrific, and when the home team did score a goal, we heard about four minutes later the cheers of spectators who must have been nearly a mile away. Apparently news of the goal had only just reached them.' [22]

Prior to the All-India match and in the presence of a record attendance of 55,000 the tourists were introduced to His Excellency the Governor of Bengal, Sir John Anderson (who returned to England in 1937 and after a spell as Home Secretary, when he introduced the famous Anderson shelters, became Chancellor of the Exchequer), The Islington Corinthians went on to enjoy 75% of the possession, taking the lead in the 14th minute courtesy of a Pat Clark penalty. Dick Tarrant completed the scoring on 58 minutes as Islington Corinthians won comfortably 2-0.

There was an unfortunate downside to the Calcutta visit in that despite 195,000 people watching the four games, the Islington Corinthians would not receive any further payments; an important factor in continuing the tour. The Indian Police ordained that all profits must go to native charities, the result of which was that the players would receive only meagre travelling expenses and tour organiser Tom Smith would be £1,000 out of pocket. Smith explained:

'During our four games in Calcutta about 80,000 rupees (about £6,000) *were collected in gate money and I was horrified to learn later that the police had decided that we must not share in the profits. Had we done so I understand that we should have transgressed some rule in connection with the use of the public ground. I saw both the governor, Sir John Anderson, and the Commissioner of Police, but neither of them could do anything about it. I later learned that only 15 per cent of the money found its*

Left: An Islington Corinthian gets his shoes cleaned at a Hindu Temple

Left: Snake Charming

way to charity and about £2,000 went in expenses. It struck me as difficult to see how the expenses could have amounted to that sum.'[23]

That same evening the team made their way to the station to catch the 10.30p.m. mail train to Dacca (Dhaka) in what is now Bangladesh. This was merely the start of what most people would consider a punishing journey around India by rail. The team would arrive at Goalundo at 5.05a.m. and then change to a steamer which would arrive at Narayanganj at 12.30 in the afternoon. Another change would see the tourists arrive in Dacca at 1.50pm ready for the match on the same day.

The players' experiences are recounted by Clark:

'Apart from the few occasions when we travelled on narrow gauge railways, we kept the same two coaches throughout the seven weeks in India. Railways, incidentally, do not provide any bedding for their customers. Those people affluent enough to indulge in such a luxury engage a 'bearer' or manservant who looks after all the bedding arrangements. The servant himself may have to put up as best he can in the travelling hovels which are provided for such menials at the back of the train. Percy Gupta engaged six such types for our comfort and an excellent job they made of it; always closing a tactful eye on the occasions we were outrageously 'done' in settlement of the 'dhobis' bill with the bearers.'[24]

The players would spend the next month sleeping on trains and Clark reminisces about the conditions:

'At any hour after midnight we returned to the sidings for a stampede in search for what I swear were the only four flit guns in India. Spraying mosquito nets followed, dust and dead flies unceremoniously removed from out sleeper, a coin tossed for upper or lower bunks and the journey continued for some new unknown adventure.'[25]

The team survived this journey and on arrival in Narayanganj, were received by an enthusiastic crowd led by Rai Bahadur S.N. Bhadro who presented a welcome address. The game was played later that day and resulted in the Islington Corinthians' first defeat in India. The Dacca Sporting Association scored at the end of the first half, and although Jack Braithwaite was close to scoring the tourists could not equalise.

This set-back for the I.C.'s though was short lived as they were due to face Dacca again on the following day (22nd November) in a rematch. In response to the defeat Tom Smith changed the side dramatically, making six changes to the team. The only goal came in the 14th minute when Tarrant scored at close range after Dacca had stopped playing because they thought they had heard the whistle. The goal stood and Islington Corinthians could take some comfort from the victory.

There was no let up in the Islington Corinthian schedule as, despite having played on the previous three days, they still had four games to play in the following four days.

After dinner the players caught the 1.37 a.m. train to Mymensingh and were again obliged to sleep on the move.

At 5.44 a.m. the I.C.'s arrived in Mymensingh, a city famous for its educational institutions and located on the Brahmaputra river. Fortunately for the tourists they were in for an easier afternoon than they had had on the previous two days and ran out comfortable 6-0 winners. Mymensingh made a bright start to the game before the tourists took control and despite Johnny Sherwood missing a first half penalty, the I.C.'s led 1-0 at the interval. The second half was one way traffic as the tourists added five goals to their total, which included the first hat-trick by a player on the tour, namely Dick Tarrant.

The team were still full of energy and agreed to a last-minute alteration to their plans when, on the following day, they were invited to play a morning match at Kishoreganj. The team motored to the town and raced into a two goal lead after only 14 minutes. The match ended in a 3-0 victory and after the game they were presented with a model of a country boat made in silver as a momento. It is likely that the following event occurred on the way back and a real boat would have come in handy: *'Once we had to swim across the Brahmaputra, with football kits on gourds (goatskins), thanks to the breakdown of our bus.'*[26] The tired footballers then had to face another gruelling train journey which entailed leaving Mymensingh in the afternoon, travelling to Bhairab Bazar and taking a ferry to Ashuganj. They disembarked about 8p.m. and continued on to Comilla where they arrived just after ten. The team then had to sleep on the train until morning, and it was no wonder that Smith said later: *'In some countries we had long journeys each night in trains which might better be described as houses of torture.'*[27]

At seven the next morning the team were taken to the Tripura Guest House with the welcome thought of a bed awaiting them, at least for a couple of hours! The game was scheduled for the afternoon and prior to it, the Comilla Sporting Association presented an address of welcome printed on palm leaves in a bamboo casket. The Islington Corinthians proceeded to beat their hosts comfortably by 3-0, taking the lead as early as the eighth minute. Only in the second half did the I.C.'s really stamp their authority on the match.

It is interesting to note that special trains were laid on by the Assam Bengal Railway, enabling supporters to travel both to this game and to the match on the following day at Chittagong. It was reported that these trains, which would normally hold 200 people, arrived in town with 2,500 on board. The supporters were crammed into the carriages and were seen sitting on the roof, holding onto the sides and even crouching on the buffers!

Tom Smith was so impressed with the hospitality shown to his team that he was later to send their host (The Hon. Nawabzada S.I. Hyder) a limited edition club badge, one of only 25 ever made, to thank him for all his help. The tourists returned after the

Left: The Stadium at Chittagong

game to the carriages that were their homes, ready to make the overnight journey to what is now Bangladesh's chief seaport, Chittagong.

The match at Chittagong was the team's last fixture in what is now Bangladesh and was witnessed by an incredible 77,000 people at the Police Ground. The locals had made improvements to the facilities in anticipation of the I.C.'s visit, but despite these efforts many people watched from the surrounding hill tops. A tight game followed and only a 56th minute Johnny Sherwood goal separated the teams at the final whistle. Clark was impressed with the local team and he: *'complimented the Chittagong team on their spirited display, adding, the Chittagong team is as good as any side we have played in India.'*[28]

Islington Corinthians now had to face some arduous travelling as they attempted to get back to Calcutta by 29th November. The journey started on the evening of 26th November after the game with Chittagong and saw the party travel via Chandpur, Goalundo and Poradah Junction, before arriving three days later at Rajshahi, a town famous for silk. The tourists spent the day here and could rest in private residences provided for them, before defeating the 1st Battalion Cameronians Rifles 2-0. They departed at 9.34 p.m. that evening for Calcutta and arrived the next morning, spending the day at the Grand Hotel.

At this point the team were in the middle of the Bengal part of the tour and the following accounts show that they had more to deal with than just football and travel:

'Their visit to Bengal was the most dangerous part of the Indian Tour, he (Smith) *remarked, on account of the ease with which malaria, typhoid and hookworm, amongst other things could be contracted. 'After warning the players to take great care. I went and caught malaria, myself,' he added amid laughter.*

At one place in Northern India where they played there were only two other white men, a Government Collector and a Police Officer, since it was situated in jungle country.

78

Left: A taxi Bengal style

'They could not find suitable accommodation for us all,' he continued, 'so the boys had to sleep in tents on the edge of the jungle which was infested with tigers and other wild animals.

'On the first night there one of the players woke me up in the early hours and confessed that he could not sleep because of the jungle noises. I had to change places with him and allow him to spend the remainder of the night in the bungalow where I had been comfortable ensconced. It was because of this, having to walk out in my pyjamas at night, that I caught malaria.'

Rot. Smith concluded by recounting how they were invited to witness the trapping of wild elephants whilst they were guests of the Maharaja.'[29]

The tourists travelled to Berhampore in time for their match on 30th November 1937. The I.C.'s won a fast and interesting game 3-1 against the Wheeler Memorial Shield Association XI, thanks to goals by Braithwaite, Read and J.W. Miller. Then it was on to Baripada, the capital of the Peacock State of Mayurbhanj, which is where they were to have their encounter with elephants.

The players were having adventures beyond their wildest dreams, and it is known that they spent two days as guests of the Maharajah of Mayurbhanj, and were taken on an elephant hunt. The object was to capture the great beasts alive, but hunting was now a rare event as the price of an elephant had dropped to £30. Clark recounted:

Right: Islington Corinthians go Elephant riding

Left: Wild elephants caught on the hunt

Right: A.J. Martin makes friends with a cat

'The Maharajah invited us to the Keddah but some of the romance evaporated from the quest when an ancient wooden-seated bus arrived to collect us at 5.30 one dismal dark morning. After a five hours' run to the foothills of a mountain range, we struck the really thick jungle. Of course, the boys couldn't resist a plaintive request to the jungle to produce a tiger with 'Where's that tigah? Where's that tigah?''

*There was not a great deal to be seen, for by the time we reached the scene of operations the elephants had been imprisoned. During the Keddah every available man in the State arrived in all sorts of garb and with every kind of noise-provoking instrument. They encircled the elephant territory and with a din like hell let loose advanced towards the stockade in the centre. This was a veritable fort built from tree trunks and camouflaged to be unrecognizable from the surrounding jungle. 'Stool pigeons (tame elephants) were driven out into the jungle to meet the advancing herd and at sufficient distance turn tail and advance through the prepared clearing to the stockade. Driven by the beaters and given the lead by the tame elephants the herd crashed its way into the stockade where heavy drop doors descended to imprison them. Young animals are sold to circuses and the bigger, older ones are trained for heavy labour.'*30

The Maharajah had a palace to the southwest of Calcutta, which included a private aerodrome complete with five aircraft, 30 cars including several Rolls Royces and an Isotta-Francini (an expensive Italian sports car). The I.C.'s were lucky enough to be allowed to use some of this vast fleet of cars.

Despite all these distractions, on 2nd December the Islington Corinthians secured a 1-0 win over Mayurbhanj with the hosts missing a penalty. The attendance for this game was a disappointing 3,000 and could have been the scene for the following episode:

*'Then there was the time in Bengal, India, when the gate suffered because 3,000 native Hindus remained outside the box office and used periscopes to watch the game. By dominion law in India, fences surrounding athletic fields must not exceed six feet in height, so the natives hung mirrors on sticks and observed proceedings from outside without paying a farthing.'*31

The tourists were now heading slowly towards North West India and were due to play five games in five days en route to Lucknow. It is appropriate, given all the hours that were spent on trains, to include the following story as told by Clark:

'In one station we were awakened by a terrific commotion of noise and bustle. On opening three layers of window wood, glass and screen, we saw a beautiful young Indian woman being carried on a stretcher to an improvised ambulance. Sure enough Percy was there, in pyjamas covered by a macintosh, to investigate the sensation. It transpired that owing to the evening warmth the lady had, at the previous station, opened the offside window for a breath of air. She had dozed off with her hand hanging

81

Left: Golf at Hazaribagh

over the window sash. Some tough denizen of the night, seeing a hand so well adorned with valuable rings, and finding no other means of helping himself, had calmly grabbed her wrist and with a quick flash of his knife removed the fingers, rings and all. The victim fainted and nothing was heard of the assailant.'[32]

On 3rd December the tourists reached Kharagpur and defeated the Bengal Nagpur Railway 3-1. The I.C.'s took the lead after 20 minutes through a Tarrant header, and the same player added another in second half, before the hosts pulled a goal back. The railway team rallied and desperately attempted to equalise, but Len Bradbury was on hand to secure the victory with a third goal.

An overnight train ride saw the tourists arrive in Hazaribagh the following day in time for breakfast. The opponents here were once again the Indian F.A. and Sonny Avery scored the only goal of the game. Each member of the Islington Corinthians subsequently received a handsome cup and cigarette case from their hosts to commemorate the occasion. The I.C.'s had time to slip in a game of golf and get a good night's sleep, before departing by car for Dhanbad at 8a.m. the following morning.

The game at Dhanbad on 6th December was a low-key affair which ended in a goal-less draw. After dinner the players went back to their carriages and slept on the train which travelled overnight to Jamalpur, a town established during the British Raj, with the Railway Institute being the cultural hub. It was huge centre which included its own movie theatre, six lane swimming pool, four tennis courts, two billiard rooms and a bowling green. It attracted workers from all over the East India Railway. The Islington Corinthians secured a 2-1 victory over the railwaymen; Tarrant and Bradbury scoring the goals. The final game of this five match marathon occurred in Patna against Bihir, and finished in a comfortable 5-0 victory to the tourists.

Tom Smith described the events on this section of the tour (which took in the fascinating deserted city of Fatehpur Sikri):

Left: Islington Corinthians with Mr. Cousins in Jamalpur

'Rotarian Smith related that at one of the towns where they stayed the residents arranged for a display to be given by fire dancers.

A huge bonfire is started and then a group commences slowly to dance round it. Gradually the rhythm becomes faster and faster until the dancers drop out exhausted. Their places are taken by others. The amount of energy necessary for these dances so near to the fierce heat of the fire are amazing, added the speaker. These dancers were also money-lenders, a business which they carried on successfully by terrorizing the natives.

PICNIC IN JUNGLE
The team then progressed to Jangipur just getting out of range of civilization. Here they had a picnic in the jungle at the spot where there were regularly held lion and tiger hunts. At Monghyr they witnessed the results of an earthquake that had taken place some time before. The speaker explained that the earthquake was not caused by subterranean disturbances, as in the case of volcanoes, but by the gradual settling down over a period of years of the earth's crust.

A DESERTED CITY
A interesting account was given of a large and deserted city in India built by Akbar, the Mogul emperor. It was a fine city and the buildings were almost intact, although it was uninhabited.'[33]

The Islington Corinthians arrived in Lucknow in 9th December 1937 and during the course of their visit they were able to view the Residency and other buildings connected with the Mutiny. Here they also went over a monkey temple which Rotarian Smith described as *'the most disgusting place I have ever come across'*[34]

The team played two games in Lucknow, beating Lucknow Brigade (the army team) 4-1 after going 3-0 up after ten minutes, and then drawing with an United Provinces XI,

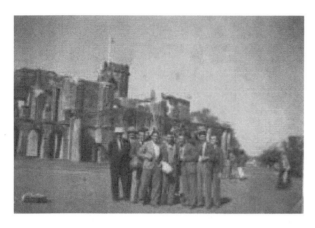

Left: Islington Corinthians visit the ruins at Lucknow

0-0, when the I.C.'s should have won on the balance of play. Following the second game the Islington Corinthians travelled overnight to Agra, where they were due to stay at the Cecil Hotel.

Agra stands on the banks of the Yamuna River and is of course the location of the Taj Mahal, one of the seven wonders of the world. The players no doubt marvelled at the structure completed in the year 1653, for the Mughal Badshah Shah Jahan, as the final resting place of his beloved wife, Mumtaz. Smith was suitably impressed: . *'It was a most handsome monument, and seen in the moonlight it was an unforgettable sight.'*[35] The Taj Mahal finished in marble must have been an unbelievable sight, with its perfect symmetry, which had taken 22 years of hard labour and 22,000 workers, masons and jewellers to build.

Having visited the market at Agra, the team moved to Delhi where they stayed at the Maiden's Hotel. For the match here on 13th December 1937, the Islington Corinthians fielded their strongest line up and it was just as well as they were about to meet some old friends again:

'On arriving at Delhi they again played matches against the 'travelling circus.' These were three or four players who were regularly borrowed to play against the Corinthians, and they were encountered so often they were given this nickname. In the new part of Delhi a certain portion of the ground had been reserved for the erection of Maharajas' palaces. The wide avenue presented a magnificent spectacle with these fine buildings towering up on either hand.'[36]

The I.C.'s superiority was never in doubt after the opening exchanges and they took the lead on 20 minutes after Bradbury had combined with Read, with the latter scoring. The second and final goal was scored by Tarrant following a scrimmage in front of the Delhi goal.

The next game was at Ajmer and involved another overnight train journey. Islington Corinthians made a fine start to this game, going 2-0 up after 25 minutes, despite

Above: The Islington Corinthians visiting the Taj Mahal

Above: The market at Agra

Left: Open air hairdressers in Delhi

Ajmer having four good chances to score themselves. A penalty reduced the deficit, before the I.C.'s secured victory with a penalty of their own one minute before time was called. The team were on the move that night and arrived in Jaipur the following day, the rest of which was spent sightseeing. From there the team returned to Delhi.

The I.C.'s were due to face the Young Men's Club on 16th December in aid of Lady Linlithgow's Anti-Tuberculosis Fund, but dastardly deeds were afoot and an unknown party had been busy distributing hand-bills throughout the city announcing that the match would not be played. Consequently only 1,000 people attended a game (which I.C.'s won 1-0) in aid of the Vicereine's worthy cause. Clark's interpretation was as follows:

'Then, as now, relations between Hindu and Moslem were strained. On the field all sects would play together with spirit and tenacity without displaying any personal antipathy. Were we, however, playing a Hindu side – and sometimes, before getting accustomed to the different sects, we did not know which we were playing – the headlines in the following morning Press left no doubts as to the opposition.

I shall not forget either the incident at Delhi when, unwittingly arranging a fixture with one sect, we found that, due to the nefarious activities of the opposition, a gate of 1,000 turned up instead of the anticipated 20,000. On the morning of the match a 'fleet' of elephants paraded the city to publish the fact that the afternoon's game had been cancelled. The elephants were placarded from head to tail with notices to this effect,

86

and all vantage sites in the city, and on the main roads into the city, were commandeered for the same purpose.'[37]

The tourists departed Delhi on the Frontier Mail, bound for Peshawar (in the North West Frontier Province), where they arrived on the evening of the 17th December 1937. Peshawar is now part of modern day Pakistan and it was here that the team were looked after by Sir George Cunningham, as Clark recounted:

'One of my fondest memories of the tour is of my stay at Government House, Peshawar as the guest of His Excellency the Governor of N.W.F.P., Sir George Cunningham, a cousin of the famous fighting brothers and himself an Oxford Rugger Blue and Scottish International. From Peshawar station Tom Smith and myself were whisked off by the A.D.C. in a luxurious sedan, on the bonnet of which was borne an unmistakable Union Jack. The latter gave us right of way through the town. Police everywhere sprang into action with loud blasts of sanguinary blasphemy at any poor ox cart wallah who might cross our path. At the Residency we were immediately ushered into the presence of Sir George and Lady Cunningham and offered a hasty cocktail.

As it was now 8.15 p.m. and an investiture was due to begin at 8.30, a very hasty retreat to our rooms was indicated. There we were engulfed in the very last word in super efficient steam-line valet-service from two bearers whose services remained at our disposal for the five days at Government House. In far less time than it takes to recount, our dinner clothes were all beautifully sponged and pressed and our 'bath' laid on. The party at the presentation numbered some seventy or eighty, and the scarlet of full military dress was mingled resplendently with the rich hues of turbans and saris.

A superb banquet, reasonably short speeches, port and cigars followed before I made the acquaintance of as fine a specimen of manhood as I've seen anywhere in the world, by name, Khan Bahadur Kuli Khan. His black full-lidded eyes appeared soft and tender on introduction, but as he warmed to the subject of his well nigh incredible experiences amongst the frontier tribes, the soft friendly twinkle was transformed into a harsh, fiery purposeful gleam. His hennaed beard and unruly moustache positively bristled with emotion in the course of his fearsome stories. He it was, by the way, who rescued Molly Ellis, the kidnapped daughter of Major and Mrs. Ellis who were slaughtered by tribesmen in 1924.

With the departure of the main party, Sir George fell to sport reminiscences, spiced by a certain embarrassing incident during the Scotland-England rugger tussle of 190-something. Sir George was fly-half for Scotland and in the last few seconds of a drawn game he intercepted a pass. He was tearing for the line with head tucked down and ball grasped closely to his body when he was tackled from behind not more than fifteen yards from the line. Unfortunately for him, he and his shorts parted company for ever, and here Sir George reflected with a twinkle in his eye, he had to make the biggest decision of his life. 'My Country or my Honour' was the issue, and Sir George confessed that to his undying shame he decided for his honour. He lay down quickly and waited for the usual screen of players to hide his blushes. He was unmercifully ragged by his colleagues after the game. To this day he cannot decide whether he did the right thing or not.

At a late hour we retired, but, despite the sumptuous comfort of clean white linen and a beautifully sprung bed, sleep eluded me. At regular intervals I heard the tread of feet and the clattering of chains. All sorts of ideas invaded my consciousness especially since Kuli had waxed so eloquently on the methods and habits of raiding tribesmen. Wan and weary I was an early arrival for breakfast next morning and Lady Cunningham was highly amused when I voiced my trepidations of the long, long night. Leg-pulling explanations were given before the truth emerged that, due to the now regular sorties of tribesmen in their search for bona fide British rifles, the weapons had to be chained to the sentries. Should the guard fall asleep his rifle at least would be secure. It certainly took the load off my mind.

Bert Read, of Nunhead, one of our best exponents of the art of dribble, did not have the same good fortune in his billet. He found himself with the officers of the Highland Light Infantry, but the only sleeping accommodation available was in an ancient structure amid a thickly wooded copse on the edge of the compound, reputed to be haunted. One or two of the officers and boys very sportingly saw poor Bert bedded for the night, but not before callously narrating all the sordid details of the gruesome murder that had been committed there. The victim had been a beautiful Moslem girl-wife who, after several warnings by her tribal spouse for suspected infidelity (the warnings, by the way, took the usual form of chopped off toes, then fingers, followed by a slice off her nose), was foully and feloniously strangled. He eventually paid the death penalty himself at the hands of the girl's brothers, but before retribution had caught up with him she herself used to return regularly in all the sparkling raiment of her kind to moan and wail her folk songs in the traditional Indian fashion.

For Bert's benefit the boys, with the help of the officers, managed to coax Jean Ferguson, wife of one of the young officers, to put on one of her best acts – a song of the murdered Indian girl. She wailed most successfully and although she did not get Bert to desert his 'stronghold,' she did at least have the satisfaction of hearing Bert creeping round nervously checking doors and windows. For the first time on the tour Bert was the first at the breakfast table next morning.'[38]

On the morning prior to the game with North West Frontier, the tourists visited the Khyber Pass which today links Afghanistan and Pakistan. The players departed on this new adventure at 8 a.m. and it is here that Clark takes up the tale of what, to the author's mind, is one of the funniest episodes of the whole tour:

'A bus was commissioned for the expedition, conducted throughout by Kuli Khan himself. The 'road' itself was safe territory and an understanding prevailed that tribesmen would never fire across it, though one never knew what would happen should the burning questions of land, love and lucre crop up. Proudly marched the

Left: The limit of British India

Left: The entrance to the Khyber Pass

Right: Islington Corinthians at the North West Frontier

Above: The Khyber Pass

tribesman who could sport a rifle on his shoulder, but prouder still strutted the tribesman with young son perched on shoulders. Occasionally we caught the flash of a rifle on some tiny rugged fort high on the mountain side. No firing was heard, however, but goaded by yarns from Kuli the boys became highly apprehensive as we travelled deeper into 'no man's land.'

As we neared the end of the outward journey the bus ground its brakes to a hasty and abrupt stop on the command of Kuli. 'Did anyone hear a shot?' he queried anxiously. Yes, one or two of the lads had heard something. Soon a turbaned head showed over a cluster of rocks, then another, and another, until the place seemed to be swarming with tribesmen. Kuli ordered us to dive for it. Some got under the bus, others to the shelter of nearby rocks amidst a terrific fusillade of rifle shots. We were surrounded and a hulking brute of a tribal chief advanced as Kuli excitedly waved a white handkerchief. Consternation ruled among the boys as we were rounded up and frog-marched to the nearby fort. To our amazement we were forced into a very large, tiny-windowed room blazing with lights which shone down on what – a feast of food the like of which I have never seen before.

*The officers of the holding regiment, for it was a British fort, soon emerged from an adjoining room, laughing their heads off. It was a frame-up arranged by Kuli, through the commanding officer, with some of the fiercest looking Indians in the company. Despite the game to be played that afternoon, a reviving drink was essential. It was very interesting to learn that peace had been declared for the period of our stay, and many coaches went to Pashawar carrying tribesmen and tommies to see football for the first time in months.'*39

The match against the North West Frontier, which the I.C.'s won 3-0, was played in a much cooler climate, which suited the weary travellers. The frontier team were the first Sikh players that the tourists had encountered as Smith recalled later:

'Our lads were a bit disconcerted at first,' said Rotarian Smith, 'for they were not used to playing strapping men with long flowing beards and head-dresses held on by pins that looked more like small daggers.' A visit was made to a Sikh temple situated in the middle of a lake. The Sikh religion is a liberal one, allowing much latitude of worship, and inside the temple was a native orchestra quite prepared to play the hymns of any religion! Architecturally the building was excellent, and it was surmounted by a large gilded dome that made a fine sight lit up by rays of the sun.' [40]

Dinner was held in the usual manner after the game, back at the Governor's residence. Clark recounts an amusing incident involving Johnny Sherwood and the brigadier prior to this event:

'In the draw for billets, Johnny Sherwood drew the brigadier, a truly unhappy pairing, for if anyone could be depended on to commit a social gaffe, that man was Johnny. Harry Lowe tells the story of how Johnny, just back from the match, was sipping cocktails with the brigadier, his lady and a couple of Cheltenham-type friends. Referring to the ball to be held in our honour, the brigadier asked, 'Are you dressing to-night, Sherwood, old man?' 'Yeah,' replied Johnny, 'I'm just on my way for a rinse.' 'No, no,' added the brigadier, 'I mean are you putting on your glad rags and all that sort of thing?' Johnny paused and then ventured, 'I dunno, old boy, but I'll put on mine if you're putting on yourn.' The brigadier didn't quite explode, but he perceptibly assumed a riper colouring.' [41]

The final game played by the Islington Corinthians in Peshawar followed the next day, when they defeated the Army and Air Force 2-1 before leaving by train at 5.40 p.m. for Lahore. The chief city of the Purijat had suffered an earthquake only one month previously, but this did not prevent 7,000 people watching the I.C.'s being held to a goal-less draw by the North West Indian F.A. in a match they otherwise dominated. Prior to the game the tourists were presented to the Governor of the Punjab, Sir Henry Craik.

After a day sightseeing in Lahore, the Islington Corinthians began to play their way back to Calcutta in time for Christmas. Late on 22nd December 1937, the team reached the Benares Cantonment on the banks of the Ganges river, a place that is considered holy by Hindus, Buddhists and Jains. The city is also called Kashi or 'the luminous' and is famed for its temples, some of which the Islington Corinthians would visit as Smith recalled: *'An unusual place was the Cow Temple, where bulls, cows, goats and chickens were allowed to come and go as they pleased.'* [42]

Clark enlarged on this part of the visit:

Left: Wild monkeys at the River Ganj

'On another occasion as we sailed on the Ganges, taking in the true India there on the banks, with the burning ghats turning many corpses into dust and the Zealots drinking the filthy germ-laden water of the slow moving river around Benares, much Indian lore and custom was imparted by our host. Benares is the place where every true Hindu returns to die and if perchance he should die before reaching the correct side of the river, it is believed that his soul re-lives in the carcass of a donkey. Well, we were all duly impressed and continued to be amazed at the frightful sights which greeted us...... *As I say, we meandered slowly down the Ganges when suddenly the air was shattered by the braying of an ass on the off-side of the river. Quick as a flash, Eddie Martin wise-cracked. 'Listen to that poor bloke crying his eyes out – he just couldn't make it.'*[43]

Clark also acknowledged that a number of the players were getting bored with all the sightseeing, so their return to football action was most welcome. This perhaps accounts for the 7-1 mauling handed out by the tourists to the local team.

The next destination was Hetampur on Christmas Eve and it is here that the following episode is said to have to have taken place. It is in fact unlikely to have occurred at this point as the team did not stay in Hetampur long enough to sleep, but it is still worth recalling:

'Bill Whittaker, too, had a novel experience of finding a cobra in his bed one night when we had to camp out in Hetampore (sic). Had Bill waited long enough to inspect it he would have seen it was dead. It was planted by Dick Tarrant who had seen it killed by a mongoose in the compound earlier in the day. But Bill does not accept that angle to this day.'[44]

The match against the Indian F.A. ended 2-0 in favour of the Islington Corinthians, the goals coming from Dick Tarrant and Bill Miller. After the game the tourists were royally entertained:

Left: Cyril Longman in action against All-India

'Leaving Benares, Islington Corinthians went on to a remote village in the agricultural district, said Mr. Smith, who explained that the place was not often visited by white men, with the result that the natives all came out of their mud huts and gazed at them with astonishment as they made their way to the Rajah's palace. The Rajah, a very rich man, was determined that a football match should be staged for the benefit of all the people in the district, and as there were no footballers in that part of India, he engaged a team from Calcutta to meet the Islington visitors, who thus came to meet on the field many old friends against whom they had played in other parts of India. After the match the team was lavishly entertained at the Rajah's palace, a dinner of 24 courses including Christmas pudding and mince pies!'[45]

At 8.30p.m. the I.C.'s departed for Calcutta and despite a delay en route, arrived early on Christmas Day at the Grand Hotel. During the aforementioned hold up: *'Ted Wingfield, Eddie Martin, Dusty Miller and Co., paraded the length of the platform, draped in white sheets from their beds, carrying the guard's lanterns and chanting in unbelievable discord, 'Hark the Herald Angels Sing.'* [46]

Tom Smith's arrangements allowed for a rest on Christmas Day and Boxing Day, which was fully deserved by this stage. On the following day, the tourists were taken to the races as it was Viceroy's Cup Day:

'Returning to Calcutta, the visitors from Islington were entertained in a royal fashion for seven days, and were guests of the Stewards on Viceroy Cup Day. While in Calcutta they saw one of the spectacular religious festivals, and among the strange sights witnessed was that of Indians eating glass and nails.' [47]

The final two matches in India both resulted in 2-0 victories, the first a rematch with the All Blues and the second against the Kings Own Scottish Borderers.

The financial aspects of the tour were discussed in the Times of India and its conclusions were:

'The Islington Corinthians, the team of English footballers, leave Calcutta for Rangoon on Friday. Mr. Tom Smith, the promoter and manager of the tour in an interview said that the players have thoroughly enjoyed their Indian experiences, but there is a general feeling of disappointment when the financial results are surveyed.

Owing to some apparent misunderstanding in regard to these arrangements, Mr. Smith has to face a personal loss of £1,000. Apparently, certain conditions concerning the results of the team's visit to India had not been made clear, particularly with regard to the Calcutta visit. In the first instance, he explained, he was to receive £3,000. An offer was later made of £2,000, plus a percentage of the gate receipts. This was accepted. There were big bumper gates for the Calcutta matches, but Mr. Smith has been informed that he cannot expect a single anna from them.

He asked why and was informed that there was a regulation governing this aspect of sporting events upon the maidan. The money had to go to charity. He has received a message from England suggesting that the tour should be terminated as it was a financial failure. He has chosen to continue because he has a great financial interest. As he put it, 'I have turned a blind eye' on the message.

The conditions were not apparently made clear so far as the financial arrangements were concerned and the side leaves India full of grateful memories of the hospitality received and sportsmanship encountered, but marred by the thought that the manager at least, at the moment, has lost £1,000, which there seems little prospect of recovering.' [48]

Tom Smith, though, did not dwell on these problems and gave a very positive interview combined with advice:

'Our matches carried us from Calcutta, the second largest city in the Empire, up and down the country, and finally to a little Bengal village, and from each place we have gathered souvenirs that will be a lasting link between the Islington Corinthians Club and the Great Indian Peninsula.

We have been greatly helped by the Press. Articles and comments have been unbiased and generous publicity has been accorded. On every mile of the 7,000 odd covered by the team we were accompanied by Mr P. Gupta, whom every member learned to respect and to like, and also by Mr. Alfred A. James (Mr. Gupta's assistant).

In, Mr. Gupta, the A.I.F.F. found the right man for the arduous tasks of arranging the tour.

SUGGESTIONS

The great enthusiasm for soccer shown throughout, and particularly in Bengal, and the proficiency and keenness of many players would seem to indicate that India may soon seek to enter the ranks of International football, and here are a few words of counsel may not be out of place. Such an ambition cannot be realized until certain essentials are recognized. Most important among these is the shoulder charge, practiced everywhere in the soccer game. Again, Indian teams should learn to play in boots, international grounds being ill-suited to barefoot play.

It would be a good idea for India to send a representative to England to attend one of the courses of instruction given by the English Football Association. He would come back primed with the latest methods of English coaching and training.

One last thing. If soccer is to become popular enough to attract overseas teams, India will have to institute larger, better equipped grounds, capable of holding big crowds.'[49]

Smith went further with his views later into the trip and gave the following interview to the Malayan Tribune:

'When they reached India, the two football associations had just got together. One association was approved by the English Football Association, and the other, which was only started recently, controlled the bigger part of India. They were rival associations, and they merged into the All-India Football Federation because of the visit of the Islington Corinthians. 'So our tour to India did a certain amount of good,' added Mr. Smith.

'The thing that struck him most in India, was the enthusiasm of the Indians. The Indians – most of them were poor – would travel between 300 and 400 miles to see the

Left: Preparing for sea again

Corinthians play, and the funniest sight Mr. Smith remembered was when a football excursion train put into Bengal.

Normally the train would carry 400 passengers, but the excursion train held 2,500 passengers who sought accommodation in every possible corner. It did not matter verymuch so long as the passengers got to their destination to see something out of the ordinary in the way of football.

'I had a very interesting chat with Capt. Gregory who is at the head of the Intelligence Department in India,' Mr. Smith proceeded. 'He assured me that since football has taken a hold of the public, terrorism had decreased.'[50]

Pat Clark in his various interviews was not impressed with the standard of refereeing during their stay in India, and thought that the locals were far too individualistic, goal shy and should really start wearing boots! He continued to say that the crowds had a bad habit of leaving early if their team was losing.

Clark's summary of Indian football was somewhat more positive:

'We left India with very mixed feelings. While we admired the very sporting play of all the Indian teams we met, we could not quite altogether accept the apparent bad sportsmanship of the crowds. They came to see one team win, and one team only. That was fully appreciated when the Indian were losing. On the other hand the same may be said of the British burra sahib who quite earnestly assured us that life in that community would not be worth living if we were beaten. I cannot emphasise too strongly the truly amazing sportsmanship of the players themselves who responded immediately and without comment to every signal of the referee's whistle. It didn't take the boys too long to learn that lesson from the Indians. Be it said, however, that the Islington Corinthians generally had much more to complain about in regard to bad decisions than our Indian friends.'[51]

96

Clark continued with his impression of the country:

'Last but not least we shall remember the smells of India. Apart from the ever-pervading odour which we encountered everywhere, I can best describe the assault on our nostrils as a mixture of rancid butter, drains and unwashed clothes, hot bodies, cow dung, sow dung and smoke streaked with a heavy perfume of Eastern spices. Once, when discussing the smells, one of our Indian friends expressed his keen sorrow for, and sympathy with, us that we smelt so, for, beef eaters that we were, little else could be expected, he thought. Were our faces red?'[52]

The Islington Corinthians departed for Rangoon on 31st December 1937 aboard the B.I.S.N. Co. S.S. Karagola, following a wonderful send off. Their record given the number of games undertaken in a short space of time and the never-ending train journey, is one that they could be proud of. It read: played 32, won 27, drew four and lost one.

CHAPTER SIX

COCAINE AND LEOPARDS

The Islington Corinthians celebrated New Year's Eve at sea, before arriving in Rangoon (now known as Yangon), Burma (now known as Myanmar) on 3rd January 1938. Rangoon was the commercial and political hub of British Burma at this time having been seized in 1852 during the Second Anglo-Burmese War. Burma, though, was moving swiftly towards independence and was the least restricted of all British colonies before World War Two. In 1936 the first Burmese national took office as Prime Minister and one year later Burma was detached from India and became a separately administered province.

The I.C.'s stay in Rangoon was to be brief, and it was the usual hurried affair which entailed them arriving in the morning and having their first game in the evening. Smith later stated:

'When the team got to Rangoon, the players were not in fine fettle, partly due to the fact that they had had four days holiday as a reward for their work in India and because of two days' sea voyage.'[1]

The game itself resulted in a creditable draw with an All-Burmese XI at the B.A.A. ground, in front of a very excitable 16,000 crowd. Pat Clark was relieved to be playing in a match with a style of play that he could appreciate:

'It really was a grand affair, for it was the first sample of English type football we had met since leaving England. The boys were in seventh heaven with the knowledge that they could 'hit' the opposition for six (cleanly, of course) with good measure accepted in return. The tussle ended in a 1-1 draw.'[2]

The Times of India gave this brief report which is the only source available:

98

Left: A Burmese Temple

Left: Sam Belly, Captain of Rangoon F.C.

Left: Islington Corinthians at the Golden Shrine Temple

'Bashin, Burma's goal-keeper, saved brilliantly. The visitors did not field three of their star players and poor finishing by their forwards robbed them of several chances. In the second half, Tarrant, the centre forward scored, but a few minutes before the end Maung Ngai, Burma's outside left, netted the equalizer.'[3]

With the best part of two spare days until the next match it was now time for the tourists to enjoy the sights of Rangoon, and they duly visited the Golden Pagoda in the city. The Golden Pagoda, which the players called the Golden Shrine Temple, was rumoured to be 2500 years old but archaeologists believe it was built some time between the 6th and 10th centuries A.D. It must have been a truly impressive sight to the tourists as the entire temple is covered with gold plates, whilst the crown is tipped with 5,448 diamonds and 2,317 rubies. At the very top is a single 76 carat diamond.

One unnamed player was in trouble during this part of the trip as Clark recalled:

'While in Rangoon one member of the team was in disgrace for the first time. (I'd better not mention any names.) On the evening before arrival in port he had been dropped for a misdemeanour. It had to be done, but it shook the rest of the boys to see 'the bad boy' ride by in a Rolls Royce, doing 'a grand tour,' while they made their way to the game in broken-down rickshaws. He had the time of his life during the two days in Rangoon. Never did he anticipate that 'Coventry' could be so pleasant. In the 'country,' however, he had the misfortune to be bitten by one of the filthy pi-dogs which everywhere defile the landscape, and had to undergo the inevitable Pasteur treatment. On board the next day he got the most shocking ragging. He had only to

appear on deck within twenty yards of any of the boys to send them scurrying into a safe corner, from which would emerge hideous howls and ghastly growls. Nobody would go within yards of him for fear of 'infection' from 'rabies.' The score was thus evened.'4

Islington Corinthians' final match in Rangoon was played on 5th January 1938 against the national team. The I.C.'s, however, were not to enjoy the success that they had had in India as Clark explains:

'You see we attacked for almost four-fifths of the game. Our forwards simply swarmed round their goal area and we did everything but score. We also missed a penalty.'5

Clark, with the benefit of hindsight, later wrote the following description of the game:

'Once again we were treated to a football hurricane and, though we lost 1-0, we were unanimous in our praise of opponents for what I would call the only worthy defeat of the Islington Corinthians on their tour of the world.'6

Tom Smith was impressed with the standard of play of the Burmese and with the tourists' reception by the locals:

'The Burmese football provided by the Universities was the finest we experienced out East. It was really excellent football, played intelligently with a very fine spirit. As to the hospitality received at the hands of the Burmese. Mr. Smith remarked, 'I don't think we encountered a more hospitable country throughout our tour.'

Among the 'sights' of Burma was the famous statue of the reclining Buddha, of which some idea of the size is gained by the fact that the little finger is 7 ft long.'7

On 7th January 1938, the Islington Corinthians left Burma on the S.S. Karagola bound for the Straights Settlements. The Straights Settlements (Singapore, Penang and Malacca) were established in 1867 when the administration of the small territory (the majority of whom were Chinese) was transferred from the India Office to the Colonial Office. The name has long since disappeared and the area in question is now part of modern day Malaysia and Singapore. The rest of the Malayan peninsula consisted of nine Malay states – four federated (Perak, Selangor, Negri Sembilan and Patiang) and five unfederated (Johore, Kedah, Perlis, Kelantan and Trengganu).

Malaya was another British territory heading for independence at the time of Islington Corinthians' visit. There had been a growing pressure for this since World War One, when the Sultans of the Malaya States realised that they had swapped political influence for economic prosperity since the arrival of the British. There were several attempts to reverse this trend throughout the 1920's and 1930's, but most of these ended in a compromise, as was so often the case when the British were involved in negotiations. The majority of Malay people preferred their traditional style of rural life as opposed to working in mines or on plantations. As a result the industries which the area was famous for, such as tin and rubber, were largely worked by immigrants.

Singapore in contrast had by the start of the 20th century secured a significant role in the trade of the Empire, due to its location in the shipping routes operated by the British. Singapore was primarily a shipping port and interestingly, until 1930, its largest revenue producing item was the opium monopoly. This trade was abolished by the British after the Japanese surrender but in 1929, prior to the I.C.'s visit, all opium smokers had to be registered and supply of the drug was rationed.

The I.C.'s arrived in Penang on 11th January 1938 and were taken directly to the E. and O. Hotel. Many of the players had been greatly anticipating their visit:

'Many of us who had not visited Malaya before were certainly thrilled at the idea of coming here. Until now, Penang was only a geographical name to many of us.'[8]

Practical considerations, of course, could not be overlooked:

''We've enjoyed every minute of our tour,' said Pat Clark. 'There is no sea sickness among us on this trip as in the previous one. Some of our boys are not good sailors.' Pat Clark said laughingly.'

... 'Everywhere we went, we have been showered with gifts and souvenirs,' he said and jokingly added, 'I am afraid everyone of us will have to buy an extra big-sized bag.'

... 'I have a lot of old College friends here in Malaya in the Government Service. They are all Scots who studied in the same University with me years back and I should like to meet them again.'[9]

The Malayans were also intent on proving themselves against the tourists and had been busy holding trial games in the week leading up to the first encounter. The Malayan Tribune, however, did not paint too rosy a picture as one of these matches was described as *'one long stretch of colourless football.'*[10] The Islington Corinthians had their own problems and both Pearce and Clark were doubtful for the first match as they were suffering from pulled muscles.

The day of their arrival saw the tourists again having to rush around, first visiting the Snake Temple (which was inhabited by one hundred living snakes) and then playing Penang Asiatics in the evening. The Snake Temple was built in memory of Chor Soo Kong, a Buddhist monk who was also a healer and who, legend has it, gave shelter to the snakes of the jungle. The temple nowadays is filled with the smoke of burning incense and a selection of pit vipers. The vipers are believed to be rendered harmless by the sacred smoke, although as a precaution the snakes are de-venomed but with their fangs left intact.

102

Left: After training in Penang

Right: Penang beach

Left: Training in Penang

Left: On the road to Alor Star

After this unusual experience the I.C.'s found themselves a goal down to Penang after just 15 minutes. The tourists remained calm and controlled and within five minutes had equalised through Sonny Avery. Tom Smith rearranged the side at half-time with Johnny Sherwood taking the lead at centre forward. The changes had the desired effect and on the hour Read put the tourists in front. Five minutes later Read set up Sherwood, and the same player scored again to seal a 4-1 victory. It was reported that many of the crowd were seen leaving before the end of the game as the locals' defeat became more certain.

During their stay in Malaya, the I.C.'s certainly witnessed some strange events. Clark recalled a visit he made with Len Bradbury to the local cup final:

'An unforgettable occasion was when Len Bradbury and myself went up country to see a local final for the Sultan's Shield, in the company of that most hospitable and indefatigable schoolmaster, Mr. Nigel Rees. Just as clubs have their mascots in this country, so the Malay team brought with them nothing less than a medicine man – a 'pawang' whose magical influence was deemed potent enough to sway the tide of victory in their favour. In all this amazing regalia and facial ornamentation he was spotted close by his favoured team's goal, muttering some unintelligible incantations in an endeavour to offset the best laid schemes of the Eurasian forwards to score. When to take the field, what end to defend, and other playing details were under the astronomical guidance of the 'pawang.' Just before the kick-off the Malay captain, with his team excitedly clustered around him, was seen to grasp the referee by the shoulders and disgorge his heart, soul, spleen and every emotional concomitant of his mercurial make-up. He protested that during

the incantations the Eurasians had rubbed lard on the goal posts and uprights to counteract the efficacy of any charms from the 'pawang.' The lard was wiped off, the 'pawang' was ordered off and the game eventually started.

It was an exciting fray until the last ten minutes when bedlam broke loose. According to the Eurasians the referee had been 'squared.' So it might have been, for the Malay centre-forward must have been at least twenty yards off side when he scored the goal. The Malay linesman did cart-wheels from the corner flag to the half way line, in his excitement their chairman rushed on to the field and shook hands with the referee, but, strangest of all, when their protests were unavailing, the whole Eurasian team simply sat down on the field and refused to budge. I wonder what Mr. Stanley Rous in his hey-day would have done in such circumstances. The referee in this match was an enterprising youth. He had initiative. As he could not prevail on the Eurasians to kick-off he awarded the privilege to the Malays who immediately passed the ball to each other all the way down the field and scored again. The same procedure was repeated till the end when the Malays emerged winning by twelve goals to nil. I never saw a more 'one-sided' match.'[11]

The tourists travelled from Penang to Alor Star, (now known as Alor Setar, the state capital of Kedah), where they would face their next opponents Kedah State.   Kedah gave a good display largely due to their English-sounding goalkeeper C.I. Burton and managed to secure a surprise result with the game ending goal-less, although the Islington Corinthians were certainly the dominant side.

Islington Corinthians returned to Penang almost immediately after this match, as the following day they were due to play All-Penang. The team was extremely tired at this point and failed to produce their form of the opening match in Malaya. The I.C.'s, calling on all their reserves of strength, finally got to grips with their opponents after a goal-less first half. Ten minutes after the interval Johnny Miller broke the deadlock, although All-Penang equalised two minutes later.   Finally Read converted a penalty awarded for tripping and from this point the I.C.'s found their form. Sherwood completed the scoring in a 3-1 victory when he headed home towards the end of the game.

The tourists' next stop was Perak (which means Silver in Bahasa Malaysian) to the south of Penang. A record crowd gathered at the Kuala Kangsar Road Stadium, which included H.H. the Sultan , the Raja Muda, the Raja Bendahara and the Hon. Mr G.E. Cator (the British Resident). It was a grand occasion and both sets of players were introduced to the Sultan and the British Resident prior to the game.

Islington Corinthians had an early scare when Perak scored in the first minute, only for the goal to be disallowed by the referee, a certain Harry Lowe. After this the tourists monopolized the play as *'Whittaker, the visiting pivot, was a marvel of constructive play. His tackling and feeding provided his men with several chances of raiding the opposition goal.'*[12] Sherwood gave I.C.'s the lead when he beat his man and then

105

Left: A village in Ipoh

Left: Scene from across the river in Ipoh

Left: Islington Corinthians visit a tin mine in Ipoh

Above: Bradbury, Chok Wan, Pamadosa, Tarrant in Malaya

placed the ball out of the reach of the sprawling Toft in the Perak goal. Read then centred for Johnny Miller, who scored an impressive second before half-time. In the second half Perak pulled one goal back when Swee Meng scored a brilliant goal, but it was to no avail as Sherwood scored again to confirm victory for the tourists. The local press acclaimed the I.C.'s performance: *'Playing brilliantly and showing marked superiority in all departments, the Islington Corinthians defeated the Perak Football Association XI by three goals to one.'*[13]

The following day in Ipoh, the largest town in Perak, the tourists faced the Perak Football Association again, and despite the fact that Perak altered their team of the previous day, the Islington Corinthians still dominated. Toft, the Perak goalkeeper, saved his side from a trouncing as the tourists threatened to run riot in the home side's penalty area. Tarrant opened the scoring mid-way through the first half when he lobbed the ball into the area and Toft, making a rare mistake, fumbled the ball between the posts. In the second half Read blasted the ball past the unsighted keeper and Pearce completed the scoring in the dying moments.

Proceeding south, the Islington Corinthians travelled by night train from Ipoh via Kuala Lumpar (the capital of Selangor) where they had breakfast at the Station Hotel. They then left at 9 a.m. for Seremban (the capital of Negri Sembilan).

Left: Dredging for tin in Malaya

Left: Islington Corinthians visit a tin mine in Malaya

Left: Native life in Malaya

Left: Spectators waiting for kick off time in Malaya

The match against a Negri Sembilan XI was again watched by an impressive crowd which included His Highness the Yang Di-pertuan Besar (the local equivalent of a Sultan) and the British Resident. Local sources were highly critical of the Negri Sembilan performance and the tourists looked tired and failed to impress their audience in what turned out to be a one-sided affair. Bill Whittaker was one of the few to gain any credit and was the brains of the team. It was he who supplied the cross for Sherwood to open the scoring on 41 minutes. Bradbury scored the second ten minutes after the interval, and this was followed at five minute intervals by two goals from Pearce. Chit Who restored some pride for the locals when he scored a consolation four minutes before the final whistle.

The Islington Corinthians were soon on the move, although they enjoyed a day's rest prior to their next game. It was probably at this point that the following incident occurred which was later recalled on the San Francisco leg of the journey, hence the strange terminology:

'Then there was the time when the team was driving between Malacca and Penang, in the Straights Settlement, and a wild animal, probably a leopard, chased the motor lorry through the jungles. The animal was a beautiful creature, Mr. Smith recalls, and was faster afoot than the slow motor.

The beautiful beast nipped at the tires and leaped on the hood, but the Corinthians from North London were not afraid so long as the petrol held out. The petrol, I take it, is the equivalent of gasoline.' 14

By 20th January 1938 the Islington Corinthians had arrived in Malacca (the largest of the Straights Settlements) and were ready to face the local representative side. With storm clouds gathering, the tourists were presented to the British Resident Mr G.W. Bryant before the game. The heavens opened early in the game and the pitch soon became waterlogged, the heavy ball making accurate play impossible. The I.C.'s should have opened the scoring when they were awarded a penalty, but Pearce only succeeded in hitting the post and it was left to Sherwood, who scored with a low drive

Left: River scene in Malaya

Left: Waiting for lights to turn green in Malaya

Left: Pineapples on the side of the road in Malaya

Above: The stadium in Kuala Lumpar

some time later. Mustapha equalised in the second half for Malacca, but with the players slipping everywhere, the I.C.'s continued to attack. It was soon Sherwood's turn to fail from the penalty spot, as his effort was saved by Ah Sang the Malacca goalkeeper. Sherwood made amends before the close, however, as he headed home the winner from Braithwaite's cross.

Tom Smith later recalled his memories of the match:

'At Malacca a tropical storm broke whilst the Corinthians were engaged in a football match, but the players carried on with the game although all the spectators quickly disappeared.' [15]

On the following day the tourists returned by the 3.30 p.m. train to Kuala Lumpur, (which is now the largest city in Malaysia) to resume their punishing schedule of matches. Their opponents were the local Selangor champions TPCA, (an acronym for Tamilians Physical Culture Association – Tamil being a minority language spoken in Malaysia.) Another huge crowd gathered for a match which was described as almost devoid of incident. It did, however, get off to a flying start when TPCA took a surprise lead: *'Ismail scored in the first minute when he broke through a totally unprepared defence and flicked the ball just past Longman'* [16] The I.C.'s battled back into the game and Pearce missed another penalty, his second and the team's third in succession. This

Left: Islington Corinthians arrive in Kuala Lumpar

Left: By the boat in Kuala Lumpar

Left: Mixed team photo in Kuala Lumpar

112

Above: Islington Corinthians team after the 5-0 victory over the Straights Chinese

run of penalty misses was ended with five minutes remaining when Pearce made no mistake from the spot, one of the home side having handled the ball. This was thought to be the only way the I.C.'s would score in this game as the usual avalanche of shots on goal was not forthcoming, despite long periods of domination by the visitors.

The tired I.C.'s stayed in Kuala Lumpur for the next two days and visited a flying school before facing Selangor on 24th January 1938. The disappointing display against TPCA did little to put off the local people, and the attendance of 9,000 for this game exceeded the figure for the recent Malayan cup final. In front of the governor His Excellency Sir Shenton Thomas, the I.C.'s recovered their form and produced a splendid display of football:

'..the visitors completely dominated the exchanges and scintillating football and made the home team look like novices. Had it not been for Kum Pak's great display in goal. Selangor would have lost by a cricket score. Kum Pak was tested 26 times during the match; 23 times by the opposing forwards and three times by his own defenders when they mis-kicked dangerously in melees in front of their goal.'[17]

It was Selangor who could have opened the scoring, but they contrived to miss a first half penalty. Midway through the second half, Sherwood slipped past four defenders and then beat the goalkeeper with a low drive. Two minutes later Sherwood scored again, when he headed Read's cross past Kum Pak.

113

Malaya had certainly made an impression on the visiting I.C.'s and it was rumoured that several players were considering moving there after the tour had finished. The Islington Corinthians now crossed into Singapore and were to encounter some worried locals who felt they would be unable to compete with the tourists:

'The problem before the local footballers and the question on the lips of every football fan is: Can the Singapore players penetrate the Corinthians obviously impenetrable defence?'[18]

They were about to find out and on the 26th January 1938 the Islington Corinthians lined up against the Singapore Chinese at Anson's Road. 10,000 enthusiastic supporters were present to see the previous season's Singapore league and cup champions take on the tourists. Admission for the game had been set at $2 for the West Stand, $1 for the East Stand and 30 cents for standing. The Islington Corinthians had to make changes with Pat Clark injured and Bill Whittaker took over the captaincy. The Singapore champions were still no match for the tourists who comfortably dispatched them with a 5-0 defeat, all the goals coming from the boot of Johnny Sherwood who had a field day.

Four days later, after several days recovery time, the Islington Corinthians faced All-Singapore in a match which was played again at the Anson Road Stadium. This time though the tourists found themselves 'in a game,' and All Singapore were leading 2-0 early in the second half.

'It now became apparent that the Corinthians realized that they must not leave the ultimate result of the game to chance.

Tarrant, Sherwood and Avery got down to play serious football, which was reflected in the many narrow escapes which the Singapore goal had.

The Corinthians reduced their deficit through Avery, who beat Milne completely after receiving a pass from Read.

Correct positioning, accurate passing and well-conceived distribution of the ball on the part of the Corinthians at this stage of the game showed that they had now struck form. This was established beyond doubt when Avery scored the equalizer, which it was well-nigh impossible for Milne to save.

Keeping up the pressure, the Corinthians scored the deciding goal through Sherwood. An excellent forward line movement saw them playing in front of the Singapore goal.

Clever passing between their quintette resulted in Read gaining possession of the ball near the flag. He passed to Sherwood. Sherwood made no mistake with the opportunity afforded him to win the match for Corinthians.'[19]

Left: A Chinese funeral in Singapore

Left: A Street scene in Singapore

Left: Another street scene in Singapore

Above: The Sultan of Johore's party in honour of the Islington Corinthians. From Left to Right: J. Sherwood, J.D. Buchanan, R.P. Tarrant, A. Avery, Mrs F.M. Still and A.J. Martin

All-Singapore still had time to hit the cross bar in the last minute, but it was the I.C.'s who triumphed and preserved their unbeaten record in Malaya so far.

Islington Corinthians faced further tough opposition in their next match against the Combined Services. With ground conditions again poor, the tourists left it late, missing another penalty (Read) before scoring the only goal in the 84th minute through the now prolific Sherwood. The Combined Services put up a grand fight and this was definitely the hardest game in Malaya.

On the following day, 2nd February 1938, the Islington Corinthians defeated the SAFC XI by the comfortable margin of 4-1. The I.C.'s set the pace from the start, giving a pleasing exhibition of football. Whittaker was again the star in his role as pivot, whilst Bradbury shone and scored the last goal. Sherwood played his robust game as usual, and Manning was particularly outstanding with the able support of Buchanan. Avery gave the tourists the lead when his shot was deflected past the goalkeeper who dived the wrong way. Sherwood then increased the lead with two goals, the second of which was a lobbed effort over two defenders who stood mesmerised.

The Islington Corinthians returned to Malacca on 3rd February 1938 and the next day destroyed Malacca 6-0 at Kubu Plain, despite Sherwood not featuring in the team. The game witnessed an incessant bombardment of the Malaccan goal and after Bradbury opened the scoring on six minutes, the I.C.'s proceeded to boost their goal tally.

After a day off when the tourists enjoyed a game of cricket against a local team, the I.C.'s travelled back to Singapore and defeated All Malaya at Anson Road in front of 15,000 spectators. Interestingly All Malaya were captained by A.L. Henry who was voted the best footballer in the Straights Settlements and who won a Malaysian brewery's competition which earned him a trip to England to appear for Arsenal reserves. A heavy downpour left the pitch in a less than desirable condition, but fortunately three opportunist goals by Avery, Tarrant and Braithwaite sealed a 3-0 victory.

Islington Corinthians then progressed to Johore for their last game in Malaya. Had this match had been played in 2008 rather than 1938, it is unlikely that the I.C.'s would have been able to complete the rest of the tour as F.I.F.A. would no doubt have banned the entire team for failing drugs tests. The incident in question is recalled by Tom Smith:

'There was a time, Mr. Smith recalls, when the Sultan of Johore invited the soccer players to a bit of tiffin and cakes. The sons of the Sultan, being mischievous youngsters, dropped a spot of cocaine or some drug on the cigars they passed around to the athletes.

The drug paralysed the lips and jawbones of the players like those of a dental patient after a multiple extraction, and the sons of the Sultan laughed like anything. It was quite amusing, Mr. Smith thought.'[20]

The game against Johore ended in a resounding 7-1 victory at the Johore State Government English School, Padang, before what was a record crowd for the town. The I.C.'s experimented with their team and W. Miller played centre forward and obliged by scoring a hat-trick.

Football matters were now at an end in Malaya and a commemoration dinner was held in the tourists' honour at Robinson and Co.'s Café. Dinner was presided over by Mr. G.W. Seabridge, the vice-president of the Singapore F.A., with 80 people in attendance. The restaurant was specially embellished for the occasion and in the centre of the room was a miniature football ground with the appropriate decoration. In front of Tom Smith's seat was a football wrapped in the S.A.F.C. colours.

Mr Seabridge commenced proceedings by proposing a toast to the visitors and expressing the hope that he would see the Islington Corinthians again; his only regrets being that the financial results were not what he had hoped for, although this was just a fraction under three times the guarantee made to them! Seabridge continued:

'A tour of the kind the Corinthians had undertaken was not one to be treated lightly, and the speaker intimated that they might have done better if they had sent down an advance agent who could have studied the standard of football, the financial resources and the local conditions. The only alternative to this was that the visiting team had to depend on people they had never seen, people who gave to the game the little time that they were able to spare from the business of making a living. The main difficulty that had arisen in the visit of the Corinthians was the changes in their original schedule, which were very largely made at the visitors own request.

We soccer enthusiasts have seen amateur football at its best,' said Mr. Seabridge, 'and the visitors have shown us how poor and feeble we are. We are proud that we have not suffered defeat by double figures! We have however learnt a lesson in football, and we hope that the time will come, when the Corinthians are back amongst us again that we are able to prove that the pupil is better than the tutor. We are very grateful to you, he continued 'for the sportsmanship you have shown both on and off the field. You have taken what has come to you with the cheerfulness that is the mark of true British sportsmen.'[21]

Mr Smith replied and congratulated the Singapore Amateur F.A. for the business-like manner in which all details connected with the I.C.'s visit to the Colony had been attended to.

'If I was a business man I would never have undertaken this tour,' said Mr. Smith, 'but I had been thinking things over for quite a long time and I was of the opinion that it was time a tour of this nature should be undertaken.'[22]

Smith went on to offer their hosts constructive criticism stating that they needed to improve their positional play, build stadiums for football, and implement a coaching strategy to develop players from an early age.

'Unashamed' of the Malayan Tribune offered his summary prior to the last game and showed regret that the tourists were leaving:

'Might I as an ordinary member of the football following public of Singapore say how delighted all of us must feel at being given another opportunity of viewing the grand team of the above in action next Sunday.

In spite of the feast, of wonderful football which they have so tirelessly served up to us under the most gruelling conditions, the attendances at their matches have not been any too wonderful in response. Lest it should also be true that the hospitality extended to our visitors off the field has left something to be desired, let us at least make some amends by rallying round and turning up in our thousands next Sunday so that the little added gate money may contribute further to their enjoyment, which they so richly deserved, during their world trip in return for the unbounded pleasure they have given to all true lovers of football at its best.

Left: The Islington Corinthians amuse themselves onboard the S.S. Aramis

'Of a well balanced side it is invidious to single out any one for special mention but who will easily forget the outstanding displays of their vice-captain, Whittaker; the wizardry, which it is the only was to describe, of their inside forwards and right wing and tireless work of their halves, who have had the good fortune to see them play?

It is no exaggeration to say that the almost perfect pattern of their teamwork on the field has been a revelation to local soccer – 'fans' and it is certainly easy to believe that on their present form they are the equal of any amateur soccer side in England. It is sad to think that it may be many years before we may ever see the like again in Singapore.'[23]

On 9th February 1938, the Islington Corinthians embarked aboard the S.S. Aramis bound for Saigon. Johnny Miller stayed on in Singapore as he had to take the newsreels of the opening of the Singapore Naval Base, and he played a game for S.C.C. in Singapore before leaving to rejoin the rest of his team mates. The players had fond memories of their visit and it was fortunately a vast improvement on what they had been expecting:

'Malaya had taken the Corinthians by surprise. Mr. Smith went on. The players had expected Malaya to be a tropical country, full of diseases, trials and troubles, but on the contrary, they had found the peoples here very kind. The climate here was not unlike that of summer in England.'[24]

CHAPTER SEVEN

OPIUM DEN RAIDS AND RICKSHAW RACING

Islington Corinthians' next destination was Saigon, which is now known as Ho Chi Minh City in modern day Vietnam. In 1938, however, it was the capital of the French colony of Cochinchina. (This and the neighbouring four protectorates held by France became the Union of French Indochina in 1887). Saigon had been captured by the French in 1859 and their influence in the area expanded from this point. Discontent was slowly growing in the region and the Indochinese Communist Party (ICP) led by Ho Chi Minh was rapidly becoming influential. The ICP were nevertheless handicapped in their quest for independence as Moscow insisted for political reasons that they did not undermine French rule.

Two years prior to the Islington Corinthians arrival in May 1936, the ICP had been granted semi-legal status by a Popular Front government in France, who released large numbers of political prisoners from Vietnamese jails as part of this process. The French never really enjoyed full control of the Union of French Indochina as the following statistic highlights. In 1925, 5,000 British officials governed 300 million Indians; by contrast 5,000 French officials managed just 20 million Indochinese.

The industries which were the source of French interest in the region, mainly rice and rubber, witnessed forced labour and appalling conditions for the local workers. It was said that rubber workers were so blighted by malaria, dysentery and malnutrition that at one Michelin company plantation 12,000 out of 45,000 employees died between 1917 and 1944. This frustration came to the fore in the 1920's when René Bazin was murdered by Vietnamese nationalists for recruiting workers through native slave agents in a manner reminiscent of the abduction of black slaves by African tribal chieftains.

The French did, however, contribute to the architecture of the city and constructed a number of classical western-style buildings which led to Saigon acquiring the names *'the Pearl of the Far East'* and *'Paris in the Orient.'*

Autographed picture of the Islington Corinthians football team which arrived here yesterday and will be engaged in four matches at Caroline Hill during their stay. Standing:—R. F. Tarrant, L. Bradbury, R. M. Manning, E. Wingfield, G. W. Dance, C. E. Longman, A. J. Martin, G. W. E. Poole, H. Lowe (trainer). Seated:—A. D. Buchanan, W. Miller, F. B. Clark (Captain), Thomas Smith (Manager), J. K. Wright, J. W. Sherwood, A. Avery. Seated on ground:—J. C. Braithwaite and H. C. Reid.

Islington Corinthians Arrive In Colony

BRIGHT SUNSHINE TO GREET HAPPY TEAM OF AMATEUR FOOTBALLERS

The Islington Corinthians arrived in the Colony yesterday by the m.s. Aramis and were greeted at the wharf by a delegation from the South China Athletic Association, headed by Mr. Wong Ka-man, officials from the Hong Kong Football Association and Capt. Neill, representing the Army Sports Board.

Above: Newspaper cutting published following the Islington Corinthians arrival in Hong Kong

For the Islington Corinthians, Saigon was just another interesting place at which to stop off on the way to their primary objective of Hong Kong and they only stayed for four days. The tourists arrived on 11th February 1938 and were met by hundreds of Vietnamese who lined the quayside. The locals had prepared a huge banner displaying the words *'Hearty Welcome to the Islington Corinthians.'*

Left: Boats in Hong Kong harbour

Left: Entering Hong Kong harbour

Left: Hong Kong at night

Above Left: Chinese street festival in Hong Kong

Above Right: The dance of the Dragon

The first game was played on the day of their arrival against a Saigon Select XI under floodlights and ended goal-less. The following day the Islington Corinthians faced the same team, and after being held 2-2 at the interval, the team scored three second half goals to run out 5-2 victors; Tarrant scoring an impressive four goals. The third game in three days saw the tourists defeat All-Cochin China by a lone goal scored by Sonny Avery. The stopoff was a costly one as both Read and Sherwood picked up injuries as a result of the rough and robust style of football played in the region. It was said that the worst refereeing on the whole trip was witnessed here.

On 16th February 1938 the Islington Corinthians arrived at Hong Kong on board the S.S. Aramis. Hong Kong had been under British Control since the Treaty of Nanking in 1847, with the addition of the New Territories acquired by a lease of 99 years on 9th June 1898 under the Treaty of Peking. Hong Kong became a free port and was intended to serve as a key trading post of the British Empire. By the time of the tourists' visit, Hong Kong with a population of one million had received the first wave of what was eventually to amount to 700,000 Chinese refugees fleeing the Japanese invasion of their homeland. This amongst other conditions was noted by Pat Clark:

'A lot else could be told of our visit to Hong Kong, city of impoverished and emaciated refugees, alongside luxurious hotel lounges, and rickshaw boys who were liable to fall down dead in their shafts after completing seven years in their vocation.'[1]

The Islington Corinthians received another warm welcome from their hosts and the players themselves were thrilled to be starting one of the most eagerly anticipated parts of their tour. They were met at the dock by Lee Wai Tong, who was the captain of the 1936 Chinese Olympic team, and taken to the Peninsula Hotel in Kowloon which was to be their base for the next two weeks. The football community of Hong Kong were

123

Above: Hong Kong racecourse on Derby day

Above Right: Chinese race goers at the Derby

to be enthusiastic hosts and the entertainment started almost immediately with a tea party held at the Hong Kong Hotel.

The celebrations continued, and the tourists were invited to fire the first gun from the new fortifications built around the harbour in Hong Kong. During the stay there they were also to be taken to a Chinese festival and a local farm. Their third day in Hong Kong was Derby day and the tourists were taken to see the race, as recalled in the following article:

'Hong Kong – Martin Loses Shirts

Members of the Islington Corinthians football team attended the Races yesterday and they appeared to have enjoyed themselves thoroughly too especially their captain, Pat Clark and Dick Manning who were seen strolling up and down the lawn in the Members' Enclosure after the tiffin interval.

I came across the party at the end of the day's sport, just as they were about to leave and they all looked very happy although A.J. Martin said that he had 'bought four nice ready-made silk shirts in Hong Kong but he had lost them all trying to pick a winner!'[2]

The first football match took place on 19th February 1938 against the South China Athletic Association at Caroline Hill. South China had made up the large majority of the Chinese Olympic team in 1936 and this was an eagerly awaited clash, with season tickets being available for all four of the scheduled matches. Prior to the game the team was presented to the Governor of Hong Kong as a record crowd streamed into the stadium.

Left: The Chinese watch from the hill known locally as Geezer's View

South China were to give a nervous performance, failing to produce their normal league form and allowing the Islington Corinthians to dominate the encounter. It was only poor finishing that kept the score down, as the I.C.'s gave the locals a taste of orthodox British football with their style and positioning. The only goal of the game came ten minutes after half-time, scored by Avery. There was evidently a minor dispute about the type of ball to be used as Tom Smith made the following speech shortly after the opening game:

'There is one matter upon which I should like to touch, and that is about the ball. We are familiar with the balls that are used in England, and we had heard that out East the grounds were hard and the balls light. We are out to give a demonstration of the game as played in England and for such we had to use the kind of ball we're used to. In India some of the balls were totally unfit for play. Now that we have shown you what we can do with our ball, we are perfectly willing to play with yours. (Laughter).

I must pay tribute to the sportsmanship of Mr. Lee Wai-tong and the others of the Chinese team. Just before the game last Saturday when Mr. Lee came into our dressing room and said that his team was willing to play with our ball, I thought that was a perfect example of true sportsmanship.'[3]

The following day the I.C.'s met the Combined Services, again at Caroline Hill. The attendance dropped from the previous day due to the rain which fell all morning, although the covered stands were fairly well patronised, but only a handful of brave

Left: Islington Corinthians cricket team against Kowloon

spectators huddled together on the open terraces. The I.C's performance also was not as good as the previous day, although they were not overstretched.

The tourists started at lightning pace and W. Miller had a goal disallowed after just two minutes. Three minutes later Bradbury fastened on to a cross by Pearce and proceeded to weave his way through the Services defence, before beating the goal keeper, Church. This was followed by Pearce hitting the post before, on 18 minutes, Tarrant increased the lead when he headed home Pearce's corner. The tourists eased off after this and only added a third through Pearce in the second half, which was followed by a consolation goal for the Services.

Five football-free days were the tourists' reward for their two victories. It is at this point that Mr. Smith probably undertook his trip to Canton in order to have lunch at the Rotary Club. Smith recalled it was *'a harrowing experience on the train journey which took 19 hours instead of the usual three on account of a Japanese bombardment of the line. Canton was the subject of air-raids during his short stay and he saw the terrible effects of the high explosives dropped.'4* This journey would have left Smith with no illusions as to what dangers the Islington Corinthians were about to be exposed.

On the Wednesday 23rd February, it was arranged to play cricket against Kowloon Cricket Club. The tourists secured another victory albeit in a different sport (by seven wickets) as Kowloon were all out for 65. Sonny Avery took 5 wickets for 15 runs and Whittaker top scored with 63 for the I.C.'s who opened the batting and scored 174.

The following evening a dinner was held by the Hong Kong Football Association in honour of the Islington Corinthians who were again making a good impression and fast gaining new friends. The Vice-President of the Hong Kong F.A., Mr. J. Ralston, made the following address:

'This month in Hong Kong history has been made. For the first time a full football XI with reserves has landed on our shores. In the present atmosphere of tension I almost

Left: Repulse Bay in Hong Kong

instinctively used the words 'invaded our shores'; but, in any case, In view of what we have already seen of their prowess and ability they seem to be going to prove all conquering force.

...The brilliant and inspiring play of our visitors has filled us with admiration. It would be invidious to single out individuals in a team that played as one. The benefits derived from the games we have seen have been appreciated by all of us. It has been a rich experience for our local players, our spectators and I hope our guests as well. The results of such an unprecedented experience are imponderable – they do not yield to statistical measurement. We all have to learn tolerance of tactics combined with appreciation of novel and successful technique. The real fruits however, are the vivifying and inspiring assurances that, under the same old flag we all play the same old game.'[5]

Tom Smith in his reply touched upon the finances of the Islington Corinthians, and gave this interesting insight:

'We have had a lot of trouble with finance. I have had to call on many of my friends and now I am afraid I have lost them. I admit that I am a poor business man, but I have the satisfaction of knowing that the tour has been an unqualified success. Success, not only in playing but in the splendid way in which the boys of my party have behaved off the field. Our idea was to show that we were not 'pot-hunting,' but giving a demonstration of the game as played in England. The boys have been such good mixers that they have left nothing but friendship wherever they have been.'[6]

The finer details were explained in the next day's '*South China Morning Press*,' which gave the true picture of how the finances on this section of the tour were operated:

'The financial part of the Islington Corinthians visit to the Colony is causing some wide conjecture. I for one was surprised when I learned the other day that all the Corinthians were receiving from Hong Kong was a guarantee of £450, or roughly

$7,000. This was the minimum figure which was offered to, and accepted by the South China Athletic Association. It allows no excessive profit for the visitors, and seems a small sum. However, after some consideration of South China's side of the question it is not so surprising. First let it be remembered that the guarantee was the figure submitted by the Corinthians, and it is presumed, if calculations were right that it would cover expenses.

Let us consider South China's position. The four matches were insured for something around $25,000 which is a figure that might have been reached with full attendances at every game. Last Sunday it rained, but not sufficient to merit canceling the match, and consequently the gate receipts were only about one quarter of what was expected. Allowing for that, a total estimate would now be about $20,000 [for the four games – ed.]. In connection with the football ground itself, I believe the stands were extended to accommodate the crowds at a cost of two or three thousand dollars. The deduction of another ten per cent for tax leaves a figure of fifteen thousand. The cost of entertaining the visitors, including the hotel, approximates $3,000, which leaves $12,000 of the estimate, of which $7,000 is the Corinthians. From the remaining sum, fifteen hundred dollars is set aside for the official dinner, which was not included under entertainment. Further incidents connected with the ground (ticket collectors, ushers, etc,) swallow another thousand dollars.

It can thus be seen that if the weather holds out for the week-end and full attendances are recorded, the profits from the games might amount to some two thousand dollars. Quite a lot, therefore, still depends upon the weather and the public support.'[7]

A weekend of matches started on Saturday 26th February 1938 with a game against the Civilians. The tourists welcomed back Johnny Sherwood from injury and he responded by scoring a hat-trick in a comfortable win. The Islington Corinthians only found their form towards the end of the 3-1 victory, but fortunately their opponents offered only feeble resistance.

On Sunday Islington Corinthians faced All Hong Kong, in the last of the four original scheduled games. A large crowd gathered and witnessed an entertaining struggle which opened in dramatic fashion. In the first minute All Hong Kong hit the crossbar and then the crowd went delirious as Fung King-cheong scored from the loose ball. The Islington Corinthians rallied well and equalised after a quarter of an hour when Read crossed to Sherwood who volleyed on the turn past the helpless goal-keeper. This was followed quickly by a second goal by the tourists when Read scored with a well placed lob. In the second half the I.C.'s dominated and proceeded to add three goals to their total through Sherwood and a brace by Avery to complete a convincing score-line which was perhaps a little harsh on Hong Kong.

The following day the Islington Corinthians made the short trip to the Portuguese Colony of Macao. Macao had been settled by the Portuguese in 1557 and was granted sovereign rights in 1887. It had become somewhat notorious for licensed gambling and opium and was considered by many as a less than desirable place. Pat Clark later gave a colourful account of the team's experiences:

'Macao has been called a 'jewel in the ocean,' but actually it houses most of the pirates, smugglers, gamblers and crooks of the China Seas. Spivs, drones and eels abound there in their hundreds and the Chinese, Portuguese and mulattos, who comprise the miscellaneous community, control the police and legal executives of the town as they also control most of the drug traffic throughout the Far East. At least they did when we were there.

Our hotel was a gruesome looking place. As we entered the main door we found ourselves in the midst of crowds of Chinese coolies gathered round the gaming tables. Fan-tan was the most popular game, probably explained by its simplicity. Four squares number 0,1,2,3, were marked out on the table, on which also was a pile of bone counters. The croupier, stripped to the waist, and a scoundrel if ever there was one, having declared all further betting void, withdrew a small pile of counters with his rake. From this pile groups of four were removed in turn until either 0,1,2,3 counters were finally left. All bets in the winning square were then paid off at 2-1. But what amazed us most was the way the coolies forecast the winning number. While the pile might be still quite considerable, two fingers would be raised immediately in Churchill sign intimating to the crowds on the balcony that two counters would be left – not once did they fail to forecast correctly. Baskets containing winning bets would then be hauled up by the more respectable gamblers on the balcony and the same routine continued.

On the seven floors of the hotel a wide variety of activities operated, the top floor being nothing more or less than an organized brothel, styled a dance hall. I had no sooner settled in my room with Bert Read when the door burst open to present Johnnie Sherwood speechless with excitement. He bade us follow him along the corridor. In his excitement to discover the source of the sensation, Bert knocked over the mysterious little spirit lamp which rested on the low table between the single beds. We reached a door which was slightly ajar and inside a strange sight unfolded itself. Two Chinamen were lying in the single beds blissfully ignorant of everything around them. Tubes from the lamp – similar to that upset by Bert Read – led to their mouths from which emanated the happiest of Chinese melodies.

To some of us this was no new experience, but an hour afterwards, just as we were due to leave for our match, an experience which was definitely new hit us amid ship. Harry Lowe tore into Tom Smith's room and begged him to hurry to the room occupied by Dick Tarrant and Eddie Martin. Not knowing what to expect Tom did as bid, to find Eddie and Dick dressed in Chinese kimonos stretched out on their single beds placidly sucking away at their mouth pieces. An inane grin of blissful contentment spread across their faces, but no efforts on Tom's part could move them from their stupor. Muffled strains of 'Danny Boy' and a sleepy 'Old Kent Road' were disrupting the airwaves of the room. As the sickly fumes from the spirit lamp choked the atmosphere there was no doubt as to the nature of the experiment. Soon the room was crowded but all efforts to revive either of them failed. Just as Tom was about to send for a doctor the 'dope-fiends' shook themselves, rose slowly with blinking eyes and burst out into the most hilarious laughter I have ever heard. They simply howled, and soon everyone was howling with them; all except Tom, who did not find the joke at all amusing. When he got over the shock, however, he was just as tickled as any of us.'[8]

The game itself was predicted to be a one sided affair with the Islington Corinthians fielding its weakest side; Sherwood, Tarrant and Avery all being omitted from the eleven. Despite this 3,000 spectators were in attendance including the men from H.M.S. Tarantula. His Excellency the Governor of Macao, Dr. A. Tamagnini Barbosa, lent his patronage and was introduced to the players before the game which was kicked off by his son on behalf of Macao. The tourists quickly asserted themselves and went in front after two minutes through Manning. Macao, however, battled on and kept the I.C.'s at bay, although Bradbury came close and hit the upright. As the game drew to a close the tourists were caught napping and Macao equalised following a 90th minute free kick.

Islington Corinthians returned to Hong Kong in time for an extra game against the Combined Police & Club XI on 2nd March 1938, which resulted in a very comfortable 4-2 victory. That night a farewell dinner was thrown by South China with 160 people in attendance, and the I.C's were thanked in the warmest manner for their visit to the colony.

Tom Smith led the responce on behalf of the tourists and was moved to say:

'I cannot remember in all my life having so much kindness showered on us before. We have had 101 splendid experiences, and we shall leave Hong Kong having had one of the best experiences of our lives.'[9]

Mr Smith then made the following people honorary members of the Islington Corinthians, and awarded them club badges: Mr T.F. Lo, Dr. S.T. Wong, Mr. Mok Hing, Mr. Ngan Shing-kwan, Mr. Lee Wai-tong, and Mr. Wong Ka-tsun. A football signed by all the players was given to Mr Wong for his son.

The events following the dinner saw the Islington Corinthians cause havoc in the streets of Hong Kong as Pat Clark recalled:

'As we descended the wide shallow steps of the hotel the usual onslaught of rickshaw boys assailed us. 'Who best rickshaw boy?' asked Dick Tarrant. They all claimed that distinction. 'All right, we'll see,' said Eddie Martin. Six of our muscle-bound types engaged the most likely looking half dozen boys, ranging in age from 15 to 40 years. They were all given the same instructions – 'You drop me first at Hong Kong Hotel, I give you dollars.' And off they went to a good start, the tapes being broken by one

rouge, Johnny Miller's boy, I think. I don't think Hong Kong ever saw such a sight before. The 'boys' were still fairly level, but some were fading fast.

Thus at the next traffic jam, Eddie was seen to dismount and lift his 'boy' into the rickshaw. With a six-dollar kitty at stake yells of protest greeted this move from the other five carriages. But Eddie was off gaining about twenty yards through his cunning. Each in turn now copied the leader's tactics, and very soon six I.C.'s., sweating up to the eyebrows in their boiled shirts, were stirring up the dust of Main Street, Hong Kong. The crowds on the pavement at first stood aghast but remained to cheer while all the dogs and kids of the island formed a rear guard to the 'Roman Holiday.' The rickshaw boys slowly began to appreciate the point. They stood in their chariots shouting their own particular beast of burden to further effort. Tearing round one corner at reckless speed George Dance collided with a Chinese barrow-boy to be submerged from head to foot in the juiciest fruit of the Orient. His pluck was amazing, however, for pressing a couple of dollars in the barrow-boy's hand, he was soon again in the midst of the fray. Eddie's guile, however, had won the day and though the protestations were many, Lee Wai Yong gave him the decision – a complete knock-out.'[10]

The final story is perhaps the best. It is not clear precisely when the episode in question actually took place, but it is certainly one of the most amusing of the tourists' escapades as recorded by Clark:

'Before leaving Hong Kong I feel the story should be told of the opium den raid to which some of the boys were invited by an inspector of the Hong Kong police. After quite an exciting motor launch trip – without lights – the party, which included the inspector, a few Chinese police with a modest sample of 'narks,' and six of the boys, quietly disembarked at one of the wharves in the roughest part of the Colony. The inspector alone was armed, but the police and boys all carried stout poles with which to defend themselves should the occasion arise. Proceeding very quietly in single file, they came to the spot indicated by the 'narks.'

It was a simple-looking Chinese restaurant. Bill Whittaker was stationed under a window at the back of the building, the others being placed at intervals en route to a covered wagon which had mysteriously appeared on the scene. The inspector gave the signal indicating assault by himself and his men on the front part of the Chinese 'eats.' We had not long to wait for action. The window suddenly flew open and out shot the most lecherous looking scoundrel imaginable, clad only in his underwear. As he fell to the ground he was grabbed by Bill and passed down the human chain to the waiting specials in the van. Six other 'scoundrels' went through the same routine. Having completed our part of the job we proceeded inside.

The proprietor was a mild looking middle-aged Chinaman dressed in the traditional style who didn't say a word while the police searched cupboards and drawers, even breaking down partitions when necessary. A few addicts lay on couches in screened off

131

Left: Four days out in the South China Sea

*alcoves, but they were so far gone that they took little notice of the activities around them. Soon the necessary evidence was unearthed in the form of a box of pinkish coloured pills. With a little 'persuasion' the proprietor produced more of these, together with quantities of opium and not a few pipes. Some of the latter were beautiful specimens of craftsmanship, which went to the boys as souvenirs of their exciting evening. Also there were boxes of Coty's 'powder' which turned out to be cocaine, sandals with hollow heels, bogus clothe rolls containing metal cylinders, bundles of faggots which on collapse revealed more drugs. We all agreed that the evening had been worthwhile – a new yarn to retell when we returned home.'*11

The Islington Corinthians' next destination was Manila, the capital city of the Philippine Islands. The tourists were considering flying from Hong Kong to Manila, but cost probably prevented this as they ultimately travelled by boat. It did, however, provide the following experience:

'Then there was the time when the team tried to board an American ship from Hong Kong to Manila, but the sailing was cancelled and they had to use an Australian tramp freighter. When they got aboard the soccer men discovered the boat was carrying a smelly cargo of circus animals.

*Great was the wonder of the British boys as to how the bull elephants got through the narrow doors into the hold until the skipper, a man of imagination, explained he waited until the elephants exhaled, then rushed them through the portals before they inhaled and expanded their chests four feet.'*12

By the 9th March 1938, the tourists had arrived at the Philippine Islands. The Philippines consist of a collection of over 7,000 islands with a population in 1939 of 16 million, which had been ceded to the United States by Spain in 1899. The Americans had set about improving the infrastructure of the country during their tenure and had installed the instruments of democratic government and a free education system with English as the unifying language. All of which would help prepare the Islands for

Left: The docks at Manila

Right: The ferry boat service in Manila docks

Right: A.J. Martin outside the Boulevard Hotel

Above Left: A coconut raft on its way to the factory

independence which was planned for 1946. It was certainly a forward thinking colonial system which had also redistributed wealth by securing land from various Catholic religious orders and selling it on to smallholders who could then provide an income for themselves and their families. It was not a perfect scheme, but it was certainly better than most.

As a result of all these policies the Philippines were described as *'the least oriental country in the Orient... The Filipinos are proud of their occidental outlook, for this is the only country in the Orient where the language of instruction in all schools is English, where the population is predominantly Christian, and where the 'national dress' is essentially derived from European models.'*[13]

It was a place where the tourists always felt at home and, in particular, the beach was a major attraction for the players when they had time to relax. The players witnessed many more strange sights including a raft made of coconuts which were being transported down river to where the factory was situated. They were to enjoy canoeing at the waterfall in Pangasinan but there is no record of their response when they attended the local Cock fights. These consisted of an endless stream of contests from early morning until midnight, with twenty cocks being killed every two hours thanks to the razor-like prongs attached to the cock's feet, which meant that one fight could be over in a matter of moments.

The tourists played eight games on the Philippine Islands, the first ended in resounding 9-0 victory against a Chinese XI, before matches against Santo Tomas University and the Philippine champions, University de la Salle which both ended goalless. Victories were recorded against Y.C.O. Athletic Club (2-0) and Letran College (3-1), before the first defeat on the islands was suffered on 20th March 1938. The only detailed match

Left: Canoeing at Pangasinan

Left: A.J. Martin on the beach at Philippine Islands

Right:
Taxi Sir? Philippine Islands

report available appeared in Hong Kong's South China Morning Press as follows:

'Alex Bolsserie, former Shanghai Recreation Club star inside forward led an all-Manila XI to a convincing victory here last evening against a formidable Islington Corinthians who were beaten by three goals to nil. This was the first defeat of the tourists since their arrival in the Far East.

Besides being the coach of the local team, Boisserie was the most conspicuous player on the field and scored Manila's third goal. Another local player who covered himself with glory, was the goalkeeper who was repeatedly applauded for his daring and dazzling saves.

The attacks of the Corinthians, who played their usual brilliant game, all ended at the goal mouth. Somehow the tourists found it impossible to put the ball past the keeper.

*On the other hand, the Corinthian's defence was frequently penetrated by the local forward line which gave an inspired display. Boisserie was the brains of the attack, and created many openings for his colleagues.'*14

The Islington Corinthians bounced back to winning ways with an impressive 4-1 victory over University de la Salle, before suffering another reverse against an All-Manila side who scored the only goal of the match:

*'Spirited football featured the match. Quinto Ortigas scored the goal from a pass from Domingo Pacheco, outside right, catching the Corinthians' goalie off balance. Sherwood missed several narrow attempts, after a scoreless first half was twice more within an ace of scoring.'*15

Mr Smith's opinion of Filipino football was that it was different from anything he had seen in other parts of the world, and that their hosts lacked understanding of how the game should be played. Smith was, however, impressed by the standard of the goalkeepers, some of whom were the best he had ever seen! He put this down to the popularity of Basketball in the Philippines. The tourists, though, again suffered from poor refereeing and it was in the Philippines that the following incident occurred: *'On one occasion a goal was turned into an off-side upon the advice of the crowd.'*16

Islington Corinthians then returned to Hong Kong for two more games which were not part of the original blueprint for the world tour. These, one suspects, were late replacements for matches which were originally planned to be played in Japan later on the tour but which were subsequently cancelled. With tensions running high in the Far East, this was perhaps the best course of action despite the inevitable disruption of the itinerary.

Left: Two players with a camera attract attention in the Philippine Islands

Left: A Philippine Island village

Right: The Islington Corinthians go native

137

Left: On board again bound for China

After three days at sea the tourists arrived in Hong Kong again on 30th March 1938. The opponents that same day were their friends from the South China Athletic Association, who proceeded to hold the tourists to a 1-1 draw. This was the 77th game of the tour and the I.C.'s were by now physically and mentally drained after playing football almost non-stop for five months. As a result the team gave a below-par performance and struggled due to the light ball used in the match, going behind after just five minutes but managing to save face thanks to a second half penalty by Pearce.

There was some local controversy at this point when Sonny Avery appeared for Kowloon in their Hong Kong Shield match against the Middlesex Regiment, the local team subsequently being severely censured for their bad form! The final game in Hong Kong was against a South China & Navy XI and in this match the tourists fielded five of their own players combined with another six from a local team. The mixed I.C.'s XI was strong enough to record a 2-0 victory with J. Miller and the guest player, Bickford, both scoring.

On 1st April 1938 the Islington Corinthians left Hong Kong for good on the Empress of Japan, bound for Shanghai.

CHAPTER EIGHT

WAR AND ARREST

The Islington Corinthians entered into one of the more sensitive phases of their world tour when they arrived in Shanghai on 3rd April 1938. Shanghai was a war zone and was currently occupied by the Japanese army following their invasion the previous Summer. Between 1927 and 1937 China had been ruled by Chiang Kai-Shek's, Nationalist Nanjing regime whose economic support derived largely from the big four Chinese banks. The economy had been stabilised in 1935 following the nationalisation of silver and the conditions favoured the propertied classes. The peasants were largely ignored and suffered both from the inequitable tax system and from the fact that the majority had only small plots of land from which to feed their ever expanding families.

The period in Japan between 1931 and 1941 is often called 'Kurai tanima' or 'Dark Valley' and it was during this time that the liberalism of the 1920's was killed. The Emperor was revered as a living god by the Japanese people, but chose to be a figurehead only and as such was manipulated by the military. Japan had been greatly affected by the Great Depression and with a rapidly growing population, high unemployment and no mineral resources of her own was ripe for the rise of nationalism.

On 15th March 1932, Premier Inukai was assassinated and this signalled the end of party cabinets in Japan for 13 years as the army refused to supply a minister for war to a government headed by a party leader. It became government by assassination as a succession of liberal and pro-western politicians were murdered because of their views. With an army controlled by nationalists, some of whom were little more than gangsters, the military proceeded to dominate politics. The army controlled the education system and all high school students had to undertake daily military training, overseen by army officers attached to each school.

The Japanese army was further strengthened by the fact that all citizens pledged to serve the Emperor until death, and with his support they grew stronger. Expansion was seen as the answer to the nation's economic problems. In particular Manchuria with its

139

Above Left: Business as normal in Shanghai 1938

Above Right: Bridge crossing of the famous Sooehow Creek; scene of much of the fighting and now the dividing line between the international settlement and the Japanese territory

reserves of coal and other raw materials was viewed as a key objective. In 1931 the Japanese invaded Manchuria and the independent state of Manchukuo was proclaimed in February 1932.. This move eventually saw Japan resign from the League of Nations and by 1933 only Italy, Germany, Hungary, Poland and San Salvador had joined her in recognising Manchukuo's existence .

Japan during the 1930's became a difficult place for westerners, as they were constantly under police surveillance and were always at risk of being denounced as spies. The Japanese themselves were subjected to an all-pervading control which sought to eliminate dissidence whether in thought or speech and a national uniform, similar to a military uniform, was introduced which all adults were expected to wear to work. The cinema and theatre glorified war, whilst radio stations played militaristic music. In fact anything western was frowned upon, including western music and dancing, and some dance halls were in fact closed. Japan was a nation preparing for war.

In July 1937 Japan invaded China (without declaring war) following a minor skirmish which was engineered near the Marco Polo Bridge in Peking. The Chinese army was no match for the advancing Japanese army which quickly overran most of northern China. Peking and Shanghai soon fell to the Japanese and in Nanjing, 200,000 civilians were murdered in cold blood between December 1937 and early February 1938. The Chinese army simply retreated into the wilderness to regroup, but casualties for the conflict which lasted until 1945 are estimated to number 20 million people.

The tourists must have been shocked to see the devastation in Shanghai, once a great economic metropolis, when they arrived on the morning of 3rd April 1938. The city had

Left: Ruins on the edge of the Shanghai Business Centre

Left: Part of the Nanjing Road which was hit during an air raid

Left: Japanese soldiers in Shanghai

141

largely been flattened during the Battle of Shanghai which raged from August to November 1937. House to house fighting ensued until the Chinese began withdrawing at the end of October. The city was a mass of Japanese soldiers and military installations and a daily curfew was enforced from midnight until 5am. The neutral Europeans who remained in the city were able to get around this problem by staying inside one of the many restaurants or night clubs for the duration of the curfew. The city was split into various settlements for natives and westerners; the native quarters were in ruins and barbed wire was used to separate the different areas.

The I.C.'s football match was scheduled for the day of their arrival and was keenly anticipated, with tickets selling by the hundreds. The local press were urging supporters to arrive early in order to avoid the rush and were also optimistic about Shanghai's chances in view of the tourists' recent defeats in Manila. The game was delayed by 30 minutes due to the I.C.'s late arrival, and things got worse as the game progressed:

'Ten thousand wildly enthusiastic soccer fans witnessed an inspired Shanghai eleven humble the mighty Islington Corinthians by three goals to nothing at the Canidrome yesterday afternoon in a match which undoubtedly produced the most brilliant football seen in this part of the world for some time.

Though the local players – and especially the defence – deserve every credit for upholding Shanghai's prestige on the football field, the defeat of the Corinthians was due entirely to their inability to finish their movements successfully. Rarely has this city been privileged to see such a refreshingly high standard of football tactics, at least as far as tackling, positional play and combination is concerned, but the marksmanship of the visitors was, to say the least appalling.

In the second half after they had settled down somewhat to the uncertain conditions of the pitch, the Corinthians completely outplayed their opponents, hemming them in their own territory for nine-tenths of the 45 minutes play. But, assisted by the brilliant performance of Willie Ward in goal, and the apparent desire of the Corinthians to walk the ball into the net rather than shoot at the slightest opportunity, the Shanghai defence rose nobly to the occasion and beat off each wave of attack with untiring zeal.

The Shanghai goal must have undergone dozens of narrow escapes in this period, and though luck was certainly not with them, the visitors' inability to score from even point-blank range cannot be excused. Time and again they had the local goal-keeper at their mercy but either drove wide of the posts or allowed one of the Shanghai defenders to clear in the nick of time.'[1]

The scoring all occurred in the first half when Shanghai's forwards raced through three times catching the Islington Corinthians on the break. Despite dominating the second half, there was no way back for the tourists.

Left: Japanese Sentries at Chapei

Left: Japanese Sentry in Shanghai

Right: Japanese troops patrolling streets of Shanghai

143

Left: A Chinese farm

Left: Shanghai coast

Left: Nanjing Road

Left: Shanghai docks

144

Above Left: Match programme for Islington Corinthians v Shanghai

Above Right: Shanghai dinner programme with Islington Corinthians autographs

Following the game the Islington Corinthians were entertained at the Metropole Hotel and during the course of this event Mr. Smith attributed the team's defeat to the fact that two tough matches had been played the previous week (although as already mentioned, one of these games was undertaken by a combined local and tourist eleven). Smith expressed the hope that the Islington Corinthians would return to Shanghai in 1940, but circumstances ultimately prevented this.

Pat Clark later recollected the Shanghai visit, explaining the players' apprehension and adventures in more detail:

'As we disembarked we felt not a little apprehensive at the sight of tough looking Japanese militia bearing fixed bayonets. This part of Shanghai was Japanese occupied territory and we had to go quite a distance before entering the International Settlement which was still more or less free from occupation.

The match at the French Canidrome was attended by Mr. Herbert Phillips, the British Consul-General, who must have been very disappointed at our defeat by 3-1 (sic). A

most lamentable staleness had set in at this stage but whether or not that was the reason I feel that lack of rest and time to recover our land legs had something to do with our failure. There was a large crowd at the game and though the Tommies and Tars were loud in their exhortations to the 'Lily Whites' to produce some goals, the heavy pitch, ironically enough, was too much for us. Post-match celebrations were naturally subdued, and most of us returned to the ship feeling rather ashamed of our poor display.

One small gang, however, nothing dismayed, were invited by friends to see something of Shanghai's infamous night life. Blissfully ignorant of a 10 p.m. curfew, the merry company went on their way. Neither did it seem to trouble them that the ship was due to leave at 5 a.m. from occupied territory. At about 2 a.m. they found themselves in a fashionable night spot, and in their usual debonair manner they danced with the 'international' selection of beautiful girls, who, for their part, no doubt, found their new type of dance partner a little more pleasant than the gigolo half-castes who frequented the place. The dancing was seemingly interminable. Every few minutes a whistle would blow and the band would start again. At last, having by this time lost their charming escorts, the night hawks called it a day and proceeded to the cloakroom for coats. As they were making for the exit a most irascible scarred-faced half-caste, dressed in impeccable evening dress, approached and presented their bill for the evening. I can't remember what it was in Shanghai dollars but in English money it was somewhere in the region of £30. To the accompaniment of loud protests it was explained that the charming and beautiful White Russians were dance hostesses and that the mysterious whistling indicated the start of a new dance.

As this was probably the first time any of us had been presented with a bill for our entertainment throughout the Far East, it was not surprising that the necessary was not forthcoming. They were held to ransom for about an hour during which time the telephone was very busy indeed. Soon a Japanese Black Maria arrived and all six were bundled inside. As the van careered through the night, its rotating searchlight sending its blinding and penetrating shafts into every nook and corner by the wayside, the boys got to work on the rather pleasant Jap officer who was grasping this heaven-sent opportunity to try out his conception of how to speak the English language. In no time he was in a merry mood, especially when his abominable rendering of 'Nellie Dean' was loudly proclaimed as 'prefect' by the admiring company.

He may have committed hari-kari for such grave dereliction of duty afterwards, but he did direct the driver to the 'Empress of Japan' when he learned we were due to play the Japanese Olympic XI two days hence. All's well that ends well, and 5 a.m. found a full compliment aboard.'[2]

The Islington Corinthians proceeded on their journey to Japan and on his return Smith highlighted the potential problems:

Above Left: Islington Corinthians morning training in Tokyo

Above Right: Ginza Street in Tokyo

'In Japan they (the players) had to 'take their courage in their hands' and play when anti-British feeling was running high and afterwards the British Ambassador told him that they had done more good than the Embassy could have done to improve feeling between the two countries.'[3]

On arrival the tourists travelled to Tokyo by train and Pat Clark recalled this unusual experience:

'On the journey from the Kobi up to Tokio (sic) by train, our eyes nearly popped out of their sockets at the sight of a Japanese businessman, in full view of the Pullman's mixed company, removing his jacket and vest and then his trousers. Calmly he took a kimono and slippers from his case, donned them, and commenced to read his evening paper. Equally surprised were we when the train attendant advanced down the corridor of the sleeper – no cubicles by the way, and no segregation of the sexes – distributing kimonos and slippers to all passengers. Quite a fuss was made next morning, however, when collecting these articles of apparel a few were missing. No passenger was allowed off at Tokio until the guilty souvenir hunters had disgorged from their suitcases the missing items. It was almost an international incident.'[4]

The tourists had time to visit the giant statue of Buddha at Kamakura and also enjoy the various local customs which they encountered. It was noted that Buchanan was certainly impressed by the Geisha girls who showed their football skills to the players! The tourists were thrown a reception by Sir Robert Craigie, Britain's Ambassador to Japan and the I.C.'s proceeded to start a 'bun fight' in the British Embassy in Tokyo, which seemed to amuse their host greatly. Clark also recalls the following incident:

Left: Cherry blossom time, Tokyo

Left: The Great Buddha, Kamakura

Left: On the way to the match, Tokyo

'Before the game our respects were paid to the Emperor at a distance of about a mile from the Palace. Press photographers got busy recording the ceremony of doffing coats, kneeling down on the pavement and salaaming flat out on the ground in the Emperor's direction.'[5]

On 7th April 1938 the Islington Corinthians faced All-Kwanto for their only game in Japan:

'The Islington Corinthians suffered defeat in their first and last game in Japan yesterday afternoon when they were beaten 4-0 by All-Kwanto. The Japanese deserved their win for after an even first half the Tokyo eleven was the better team.

All-Kwanto got a chance to score after the game was only two minutes old when Shinozaki, from a pass from Kamo, had a grand opening. The Japanese winger failed in his attempt however, and both teams fought it out on very even terms until the 40th minute when the Japanese jumped into a lead which they were never to lose.

Kim, All-Kwanto's speedy right half after dribbling the ball half way down the field, tricked Bradbury and sent a low pass over to Kamo. The Japanese inside right lobbed the ball in front of the visitor's goal and the next instant Ninomiya, All-Kwanto's centre had scored.

During the second half the Japanese completely monopolized the game, Ninomiya, and the Kamo brothers being the spearhead. According to Domel, the Corinthians showed obvious signs of fatigue and seemed to play half heartedly. The visitors had a chance to equalise nine minutes after the restart when they were awarded a penalty. Pierce (sic) took the kick but failed to score, and after this the Japanese took complete control, scoring three goals in succession.'[6]

Clark explained his thinking about the defeat:

'The Japs played a lively brand of football and fully merited their win, although I am sure that had we not suffered from staleness, as we undoubtedly did at this stage, a different score would have resulted. Three goals were in the last five minutes on a pitch which was like a skating rink. Due to rush tactics once again, Harry Lowe did not have the time to doctor our boots for the difficult underfoot conditions. While our poor display did not prevent Sir Robert Craigie, the British Ambassador, from inviting us to the Embassy, he must have felt very despondent at the result.'[7]

Clark was left to make the post-match speech, which was usually untaken by Tom Smith, who perhaps knew what was coming! Clark also gives an insight into his perception of Japan as a country in this interesting extract:

'During my speech, too, I was dismayed to hear some of my most lavish compliments greeted by loud hisses from the Japs. This was an expression of Japanese appreciation.

Left: Football in ceremonial robes

Left: Japanese girls try football

Right: Japanese children in traditional dress

Yes, the Japs seem to do everything on a system of opposites. They shake their heads when they accord with your opinion and nod them when they disagree. Instead of dressing for dinner they undress and put on slippers and kimonos. Their saws are wide at the cutting end and all houses are built from the top. Cats purr when annoyed and when dogs' tails wag it is best to be prepared. Even the headlines in the newspapers are at the bottom of the paper. We all derived amusement from the Japanese custom of clasping hands and endless bowing on meeting friends in the street. In the hotel at all times could be seen a couple of louts with clasped hands, politely bowing to each other. When we were leaving Tokio (sic) we even saw a young couple miss their train because their older relations did not cease the courtesies in time. The old folk hold the privilege of indicating the 'knocking off' time.'[8]

The Islington Corinthians then returned to the ship in Yokohama only to find it had been put into quarantine, three cases of cholera having being diagnosed on board. This became a 24 hour delay before the ship was allowed to depart for Honolulu in Hawaii.

CHAPTER NINE

HOLLYWOOD DREAMS

After a week at sea the Islington Corinthians arrived in Hawaii on board the Empress of Japan. Hawaii had been part of the United States since annexation in 1898 (following requests from the newly formed Republic of Hawaii), although it enjoyed self-governance as a Territory from 1900. Despite attempts in 1947 it was not until 1959 that Hawaii became the 50th state of the Union. The main group of the Hawaiian Chain consists of 20 islands, eight of which are inhabited. These and hundreds of outcrops in the chain include both volcanic and coral islands spread over 1,500 miles which by 1940 had a population of 422,770. The capital is Honolulu on the island of Oahu and it was here that the tourists would base themselves for their all too brief visit.

The Islington Corinthians' welcome to the island was not quite what the players had been hoping for:

*'The boys were disappointed, however, not to be greeted by bevies of hula-hula girls with carnations in their hair. Their smart American dress was a disappointing anti-climax but later a visit up country provided something at least remotely representing what was expected.'*₁

The game which followed was without doubt the most one-sided affair of the whole world tour and ended in a resounding victory for the I.C.'s. The headline tells the whole story:

CORINTHIAN GOAL TENDER WASTED AFTERNOON IN TOWN

OAHU ALL STARS 0 ISLINGTON CORINTHIANS 10

'Ted Wingfield of the Corinthian soccer team of London, England wasted an afternoon in Honolulu yesterday.

Right: Pearce and Avery in Honolulu

Left: Waikiki Beach taken from hotel window

Right: On the beach at Honolulu

Mr. Wingfield could have enjoyed Hawaii's salubrious climate and taken in some of the scenery.

A peek over the Nuuanu pali or a spin through the pineapple layout would have been more profitable as far as Mr. Wingfield is concerned.

Or Mr. Wingfield, had he been too seasick to get around, could have spent the time catching up with the world's news events in the library or even on the deck the Empress of Japan on which he and his team mates are travelling.

For Mr. Wingfield of London is the goal tender of the Islington Corinthians team, amateur 'hoot mon' champions of all England.

And as goalie for the world touring Corinthians yesterday Mr. Wingfield had nothing to do.

In fact, he would have dozed off in deep slumber had not his team mates on occasions, booted the ball back to him just to see if he was on the job.

DIDN'T SEE ACTION
The Corinthians backs and forwards were busy scoring goals, 10 of 'em, against the Honolulu All-Stars that not once in the entire exhibition did Mr. Wingfield was called upon to make a real save (sic).

He could have called for a chair and umbrella and camped under the nets, and imagined he was on the beach at Waikiki with the surf rolling up to his feet.'[2]

The tourists simply cruised into a six goal lead by half-time, as H.C. Read led the way with four goals.

The touring Islington Corinthians were fascinated by the surf-boards they encountered on Waikiki beach and described them as large planks of wood! The I.C.'s were to spend only a couple of days in Hawaii before departing for the United States mainland.

The Islington Corinthians spent five days at sea, before arriving in Los Angeles at 10am on 21st April 1938 for what was undoubtedly the highlight of the trip in the eyes of the players. The tourists were treated like Hollywood stars from the very beginning and were whisked away from the port, accompanied by a police escort with sirens screaming, directly to City Hall to meet the Mayor of Los Angeles.

America was recovering slowly from the Great Depression which had followed the Wall Street Crash in 1929, although at the time of the I.C.'s arrival it had entered a recession in which unemployment reached 19%. It was the era of isolationism as the United States endeavoured to stay neutral and avoid being dragged into another

Above: Joan Woodbury and Charles Boyer on the set of Algiers with Johnny Miller and Jack Braithwaite

Left: Islington Corinthians with David Niven and Charles Boyer

European war. Despite the economic problems, Hollywood had emerged as the movie capital of the world.

It was beyond the wildest dreams of the players to be rubbing shoulders with world famous movie stars during their stay, but that is precisely what happened. The tourists went to Hollywood and were taken around all the major film sets. At Warner Bros. Studios, they were introduced to the down to earth Charles Boyer who was playing his most famous role, Pepe le Moko, the thief on the run, in *'Algiers,'* for which he received an Oscar nomination. Another actor they encountered on the film set of *'Algiers'* was Maltese actor Joseph Calleia, who was also famed for his singing and composing, both on Broadway and in film. During their visit to the Technicolor studios of Warner Brothers, the tourists were taken around the film set of *'The Adventures of Robin Hood,'* which starred Errol Flynn.

Perhaps the most famous actor the tourists met was David Niven who was filming *'Five Blind Mice,'* with Charles Farrell at 20th Century Fox. The latter was a future mayor of Palm Springs and is best remembered for his onscreen romances with Janet Gaynor in more than a dozen films including *'Seventh Heaven.'* David Niven, rather appropriately in view of the Islington Corinthians' exploits, was subsequently best known for his role as Phileas Fogg in the 1956 film *'Around the World in Eighty Days.'* Niven too, was a Londoner (albeit Scottish born), who had joined the army and served in the Highland Light Infantry.

Left: Our host, Victor McLaglen

Left: Islington Corinthians with Pat O'Brien at Warner Brothers Studio

Right: Joan Woodbury with the Islington Corinthians after the game with Douglas Aircraft

156

Above: Press Cutting from Los Angeles

The future star became bored with army life and decided to leave the services following a lengthy lecture on machine guns which was interfering with his plans for dinner with an attractive young lady. The major general invited questions at the end of the lecture, to which Niven asked *'Could you tell me the time, sir? I have to catch a train.'* Following this he was placed under arrest for insubordination, although he claimed to have escaped after sharing a bottle of Whiskey with the officer who was guarding him. Niven left England for America and en route sent a telegram resigning his commission. By 1934, Niven arrived in Hollywood and after being an extra went on to star in *'The Prisoner of Zenda,' 'Wuthering Heights'* and *'A Matter of Life and Death.'* He later received an Oscar for his part in *'Separate Tables.'*

The tourists also visited the United Artists studios and encountered many more stars. Clark mentions meeting Victor McLaglen, another British actor, who had been a wrestler and who became heavy-weight boxing champion of the British Army in 1918. McLaglen was a popular actor renowned for playing drunks, and had received an Academy Award for Best Actor for his role in *'The Informer.'*

Other famous personalities included: Hedy Lamarr (the beautiful Austrian actress who starred in *'Boom Town,' 'White Cargo'* and *'Ziegfield Girl'* and who also co-invented an early form of spread spectrum encoding, a key to modern wireless communication), Heather Angel, (the British born star of *'The Hound of the Baskervilles,' 'The Three Musketeers'* and *'Last of the Mohicans'* and later provided the voices on the Disney films, *'Alice in Wonderland'* and *'Peter Pan'*) and Joan Woodbury (a tall provocative actress who rarely rose from the B list category, but who gained fame for a sultry dance routine in *'Charlie Chan on Broadway'*).

The list continues with Marian Mansfield, (a protégé of Bing Crosby who appeared in *'Love in Bloom'* and later became a singer for bandleader Guy Lombardo); Béla Lugosi (the star of several Dracula films); Nigel Bruce (who played buffoonish, fuzzy-minded gentlemen in many of his 78 films which included *'Treasure Island,' 'The Scarlett Pimpernel'* and Alfred Hitchcock's, *'Rebecca'* and several Sherlock Holmes movies with Basil Rathbone); Pat O'Brien (who starred in eight movies with James Cagney and also appeared with Ronald Reagan in *'Knute Rockne, All American'*); and finally the English actress Binnie Barnes, whose most famous role came in *'The Private Life of Henry VIII.'*

The film stars all made a major effort to make the Islington Corinthians feel at home, in particular Victor McLaglen and Heather Angel who received a special mention by Clark. The superstar lifestyle continued when the tourists were invited to take part in a radio broadcast live on Radio Station KZIB:

'A radio broadcast on a national hook-up was my next terrifying task, but a drink with William Powell and Myrna Loy, who were doing an excerpt from 'The Thin Man,' more than recompensed me for any discomfiture. During this spell David Niven was often seen with the boys. On one occasion George Pearce was tickled to death when David asked Bob to move and make room for George at the Douglas Match. Bob was Robert Montgomery (the future lightweight boxing world champion). Heather Angel was our chief hostess and a capable one at that. She spared no effort to see that everyone had a good time, and Binnie Barnes was not far behind. Victor McLaglan at his night club put on the most terrific spread in the form of a Barbecue. Cyril, I may say was just as lively as Victor was subdued. During a visit to the studios we had the pleasant experience of quite a long conversation with Charles Boyer and Hedy Lamarr in the filming of 'Algiers.' A cricket match against Sir Aubrey Smith's XI created much banter and good fun at the 'local' afterwards, with Nigel Bruce and a host of British stars. Along Sunset Boulevard the most amazing road and 'eats' signs greeted the eye. 'Eat at Ned's and keep your wife for a Pet,' was one. At the match the itinerant ice

Left:
The Los Angeles Coliseum

Left: The Hollywood Bowl

Left: The city gates of Nottingham on the Robin Hood film set which starred Errol Flynn

159

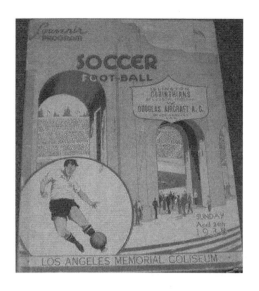

Above Left: Programme for Islington Corinthians v Douglas Aircraft

Above Right: Johnny Sherwood before a game in Los Angeles

*cream vendors would bellow 'Have an ice and give your tongue a sleigh ride.' In one café a greeting read 'Credit upstairs. Use the Elevator' There was no elevator.'*₃

Despite all this excitement the tourists still honoured their commitments visiting the Los Angeles Rotary Club for a luncheon on 22nd April and being entertained later that day by the British Societies of South California at the Riviera Country Club. The tourists were also taken to the San Diego racetrack and the Hollywood Bowl.

The first match in America took place on the 24th April 1938 at the Memorial Coliseum, scene of the athletic events at the 1932 Olympics and later the home of the Los Angeles Rams American Football team. Their opponents were Douglas Aircraft who were selected on the basis of being the reigning Los Angeles champions. The game on this occasion was open to the public with no admission charge. Douglas Aircraft proved worthy opponents and a hard fought game ended goal-less with the second half being played in torrential rain. The American team looked on the result as a moral victory, marred only by a broken ankle sustained by Douglas's Billy Martin. The Islington Corinthians sportingly allowed their hosts to make a substitution after this loss.

Two days later the Islington Corinthians faced the All Stars at the Loyola Stadium, which was owned by Loyola Marymount University. A substantial 6,000 crowd gathered for the match which generated $4,000 dollars in gate money, although the

Left: Johnny Miller in front of a tram car in Los Angeles

Right: Main Street in Los Angeles

Left: Islington Corinthians after appearing on the KZIB radio station

Left: Islington Corinthians cricket team in Los Angeles

Islington Corinthians were to receive only $70 after the expenses were discounted. Matters were not helped by the fact that Glenn Cunningham, one of the top 'amateur' athletes in America at this time (who won a silver medal in the 1,500 meters at the 1936 Olympic Games at Berlin), was paid $1,000 to appear at half-time. Despite going a goal behind to the All Stars, the tourists recovered to be level at half-time and then proceeded to score three second half goals with a *'dazzling display of soccer football'*[4]

The tourists had time for a cricket match (at the Hollywood Cricket Club which was founded by Sir Charles Aubrey Smith) before departing for San Francisco on 29th April 1938, where they were to stay at the Plaza Hotel. The city was famed for the Golden Gate Bridge which opened the previous year, and the infamous Alcatraz prison which was then fully operational, one of the inmates being Chicago gangster Al Capone.

The match with the North Californian All Stars attracted a fair degree of interest from the local newspapers and the San Francisco Chronicle previewed the game as follows:

'You've undoubtedly heard of soccer being played before 100,000 people in Europe. Of riots, perpetrated by victory-drunk fans. Of cities going goofy when their team walloped the opposition 1-0, staging serpentine parades all night and the whole town hitting the hay the next morning to nurse swollen heads.

You've heard of all that, but today will be, for the majority, a rare chance to ogle in action the players who have brought all these things about, when the Islington Corinthians battle Northern California at Kezar Stadium.

Forming the most colorful (sic) *band of soccer pilgrims ever to touch American soil, the Corinthians, seven months away from home and trotting the globe at an estimated cost of $60,000, naturally are favored* (sic) *to defeat the best of the home talent, but it should take nothing away from the game which will be an International contest in every respect.'*[5]

Left: San Diego Racetrack

Left: The Santa Monica Highway

Right: The Golden Gate Bridge

163

The game was played at the Kezar Stadium which is now the home of the California Victory football team, who play one level below the Major League Soccer. It also achieved fame as the former home of American Football teams the Oakland Raiders and the San Francisco 49ers.

Despite a close score-line the Islington Corinthians dominated the match, with the final shot count (a popular statistic in the U.S.) being 35 to 15 in favour of the tourists. The North Californian All Stars took the lead on 20 minutes, but the I.C.'s were level 12 minutes later when *the boys from across the pond equalized when Bill Miller skidded one past Goalie Wolter.'6* The tourists went in front three minutes before the interval through Tarrant, only to be pegged back again. The deciding goal was scored on 67 minutes when the I.C.'s drew Wolter out of his goal and Johnny Miller shot home from 15 yards.

The following analysis was reported after the game:

'Everything was friendly and sweet on the field as the boys handled themselves like little gentlemen. An unofficial count, however, reveals that 28 local lads landed hard and squarely on their rumble seats after running into Corinthians, while only 17 of the visitors had their dignity ruffled that way.'7

The Islington Corinthians' last game in the United States was played on 4th May 1938 at the Seals' Stadium. Long since demolished (on completion of Candlestick Park in 1959) the stadium was at this point a minor league baseball arena, home of San Francisco Seals and the San Francisco Missions.

The North Californian All Stars were again the opposition and another entertaining match ensued. The San Francisco Chronicle stated *'The Corinthians of North London, England, looking like a million dollars, between the 20 yard lines,'8* started slowly and the All Stars took the lead on 15 minutes, before a low 25 yard drive by Johnny Sherwood levelled matters. The All Stars came back strongly and scored again just prior to half-time, after Cyril Longman in the I.C.'s goal had dropped the ball. The tourists equalised in the second half, when Tarrant released Johnny Miller on the left wing, and his cross was converted by Braithwaite to complete the scoring in a 2-2 draw.

Following this the Islington Corinthians continued by train towards the final leg of their journey. Although 8,000 miles from England, the players felt at this point that they were practically home. From San Francisco they were to travel 700 miles north to Seattle, before progressing onto Vancouver in Canada. The tourists must have had nightmares about another arduous train journey following their exploits in India, none more so than George Pearce who practically ended his football on the trip following this incident:

Above: Seattle, Washington

SOCCER IN BED DOES NOT PLAY DIVIDENDS
'George Pearce, member of the Islington Corinthians, a London soccer team, let the game get the best of him in his sleep. He was treated here Friday for severe leg lacerations suffered when he kicked his foot through the window of his pullman berth.'9

CHAPTER TEN

THE FINAL VOYAGE

The weary travellers arrived in Vancouver, commercial capital of British Columbia on 6th May 1938. It was the final leg of the journey and many of the tour party were looking forward to returning to England. First, however, the Islington Corinthians had to cross Canada, the second largest country in the world, which had evolved from a group of European colonies to become the modern-day state in 1867. Canadian participation in the First World War helped to foster a sense of nationhood, but like many countries they had been hit hard by the Great Depression and at the time of the I.C.'s visit, Canada was still struggling to recover from this economic set-back. Unemployment within Canada's 11 million population had hit 25 per cent during the worst years and with Canadian car owners no longer being able to afford petrol, many reverted to having their vehicles pulled by horses. These were dubbed Bennett Buggies, named after the Prime Minister who failed to give aid along the lines of Roosevelt's New Deal south of the border.

The Islington Corinthians were not, however, concerned with the Canadian economy and arrived in high spirits:

'Islington Corinthians acting more like a group of prankish schoolboys than a crack world-touring English soccer team, arrived here last night to play their first match on Canadian soil.

...Apparently more interested in their 'bit of a game' than in their first glance at Canadian surroundings, the 17 players who left London last October, left the train singing and chasing one of their number up the platform.

Outside a large bus which was to take them to their hotel drew the remark 'they must do a lot of good travelling in this country.'

Left: Rugged scenery in Canada

Team Manager Tommy Smith, who admitted he has a 'bit of a time with my lads sometimes,' declared however they were 'different fellows on the playing field. They leave their pranks in the lockers with their clothes.''[1]

The Canadian leg of the mammoth world tour was certainly going to be one of the easiest for Tom Smith, as he had arranged for the I.C.'s to be paid 70 per cent of the gate receipts in order to cover expenses and this time had no problems with the local bureaucracy.

The first fixture was in Vancouver against the Mainland All-Stars and this proved to be one of the hardest matches so far on the tour. Starting positively the tourists took the lead through Johnny Miller after just five minutes, but by half-time were 1-2 in arrears. The score-line did not change until five minutes from the end when Sherwood passed to Tarrant who equalised with a hard drive.

Clark summarised the events surrounding the game later:

'The two goals draw in fact was something of a compliment to the Mainland All Stars. That despite the fact that Dick Tarrant was offside, from here to China, when he ran in our equalizing goal seven minutes from time.

In the Islington dressing room before the match Tom Smith, personable and outspoken manager of the tourists, practically predicted a local victory. 'Frankly,' said he, 'we don't figure to beat Vancouver. A side that held Charlton Athletic (Runners-up in the Football League Division One in 1936/37) *to an odd goal last year should have our number.' We countered our manager's prophecy with ninety minutes of exhibition football as fascinating as any visiting team has ever presented in Vancouver.'*[2]

The I.C.'s were also quickly making friends in Canada as the following article in the *'Winnipeg Free Press'*:

Left: The hotel in Vancouver

Left: National Park in Vancouver

Right: National Park Golf Course

168

'The Islington Corinthians created a wonderful impression in their game against the Vancouver All-Stars last Saturday, so much so that the officials were besieged with requests to play a return game in Vancouver, which they have agreed to do next Thursday.

The Vancouver sport scribes have nothing but praise for the display put up by the Corinthians and describe them as the finest side to ever perform in Vancouver. The writers state that their positional play is a treat to watch, and in addition they have all the fire and dash of an amateur side as compared to a professional side who, naturally, will not take any chances.

Lowe said later in the tour that this was the best team played on the tour in his opinion.'3

After visiting the National Park in Vancouver, the tourists continued their journey via the Canadian Pacific Railway which had been built to provide a link from British Columbia to the eastern provinces. The railway threaded its way through the torturous terrain of the Rocky Mountains, crossing treacherous mountain passes, fast rivers and sheer drops with an assurance that made the whole line a marvel of construction. The tourists would have been confronted by breath taking scenery as they continued homeward across the rugged Canadian landscape.

Before heading east Islington Corinthians played at Naniamo on Vancouver Island on 9th May 1938 and suffered their first reverse on Canadian soil. The tourists found themselves three goals behind after just 49 minutes, but two penalties by Sherwood gave the scoreline an air of respectability. This setback did not linger long in the memory as two days later the I.C.'s arrived in Victoria and *'used their soccer wizardry to produce four second-half goals.'4* The tourists had found themselves two goals behind early in the game, but they rolled up their sleeves and Tarrant scored twice to bring the scores level. Victoria scored a late consolation, but the I.C.'s recorded a comprehensive 6-3 victory.

The following anecdote from prior to the game with Victoria shows that despite a certain degree of homesickness, the tourists were still intent on having a good time and had not lost their sense of humour:

'Tarrant pulled a quickie on Lowe in Victoria according to the Vancouver Sun. Those who met Richard will get a laugh out of it and for others it will give an insight into the light-hearted manner in which these young Englishmen have been kicking their way around the world.

The quick-witted Dick phoned Lowe's room last Wednesday a.m. while the trainer was fixing the boots.

'Are you there?' barked Lowe, answering the call.

'This is the manager,' responded Tarrant in disguised voice. 'I say, old man, you'll have to stop that dratted hammering. Guests in the hotel are complaining. They can't sleep with that infernal row.'

Lowe, was all apologies. 'Sorry sir,' said he, 'but I've only one more pair of boots to do. Mayn't I finish them?'

'I'm sorry,' answered the emulating Tarrant, 'but you'll have to go out in the yard and do it. We can't afford to disturb the guests.'

'But, hell, it's raining out,' pleaded Lowe. 'I'll just be a jiffy. Please can't I finish here.'

'Go ahead then, you bloke,' laughed Tarrant and hung up.'[5]

On leaving Vancouver Island the Islington Corinthians briefly returned to the city of Vancouver and faced the Mainland All-Stars again (in a game excluded from the I.C.'s records); this time the home side attacked aggressively from the start and the tourists were never in the game, eventually losing 0-3. Vancouver made a lasting impression on Pat Clark who was moved to say *'To intending emigrants, may I give this word of advice? If it's to be the British Empire make it Vancouver, the finest spot in the world.'*[6] The next stop was Calgary in the province of Alberta, where honour was once again restored with a 3-0 victory, the tourists having overcome the home side's early raids.

The tourists departed the following day at 2 p.m. by bus for Lethbridge, their next destination and en route they visited the Turner Valley oilfield. The party arrived in Lethbridge in the early evening and received a civic welcome from the Mayor and city fathers. News had travelled fast and it was reported *'the members of the touring eleven are a fine group of athletes, typical of the English amateur. They are well-spoken and are 'sporting gentlemen' both on and off the field.'*[7]

The people of Lethbridge made the Islington Corinthians feel at home and next morning they were taken on a tour of the city then to a celebratory lunch with 150 guests at the Masonic Hall. The game against Lethbridge saw the I.C.'s held at bay until late in the game. The score at half-time stood at one a piece, but in the second period the tourists had the north east wind at their backs and maintained a constant attack, culminating in Braithwaite and Bradbury scoring in the last ten minutes to secure a 4-2 victory.

The festivities continued at nine o'clock with a dinner at the Marquis Hotel which which happily coincided with the Lethbridge Club's anniversary. This was another well attended event with 200 people present and some concerns had been expressed earlier about the council's use of public funds to entertain the visitors on this scale. A grant of $75 from the council towards the cost had been agreed, but this was later

Left: Scenery in Alberta

Right: Scene from the Rockies

Left: Travelling in Canada

withdrawn when it transpired the Rotary Club had already organised and paid for the event!

Smith made the following complimentary address:

'Lethbridge has given us the most friendly welcome of our tour.' Manager Tom of the Islington Corinthians, famous English amateur soccer club, summed up the unanimous opinion of his party in these words at a civic luncheon tendered the visitors Monday night.

'We are here by accident,' said Mr. Smith, 'and it was a very fortunate accident for us.' He then went onto explain how they had originally been scheduled to play in Edmonton, but that the game had subsequently been changed to Lethbridge.

'The speeches given today.' He continued, 'were the best we have heard and altogether our visit in your city has and is affording us the utmost pleasure.'[8]

The Islington Corinthians' visit to Lethbridge was reviewed by the local press in colourful terms:

'Islington Corinthians, those prankish pigskin-punters from London, have come and gone, leaving in their wake some pleasant memories and staunch supporters.

The happy frolickings of the tourists, the wise-cracks delivered in real English accent and manner, the tricks they played on themselves and their hosts, combined to capture the friendship of all with whom they came in contact here.

They were much easier to talk to than other touring Old Country clubs, displaying as much interest in their surroundings as their surroundings did in them.

They were peppered with questions, besieged by autograph hunters and kept constantly on the move. But their good humour was unquenchable and they took it all in their stride.

They were the 'life of the party' at the Rotary reception and dance at the Marquis hotel following the game against Lethbridge All-Stars.

I sat next to Harry Lowe at the civic luncheon Monday noon in the Masonic hall and really enjoyed his droll humour. Lowe is the club's trainer and a gent who patrolled the centre-half patch for Tottenham Hotspurs at one time. He is the story-telling wizard of the team with Dick Tarrant a close second.'

....Lowe was up to his tricks at the banquet too, for when one of the lads showed a liking for Lethbridge 'bee-ah.' Harry quickly passed all the empty bottles he could find, until the player in question could hardly move without knocking some over.'[9]

172

Left: The Banff Springs Hotel

Islington Corinthians moved onto Saskatchewan and at Saskatoon they displayed fine team work in winning 3-0. A feature of this game was that two of the Saskatoon players were native Indian brothers from a reservation 65 miles north of the city. Another 3-0 victory was recorded over Regina, before the tourists arrived in Winnipeg, Manitoba on 20th May 1938.

Islington Corinthians again arrived in high spirits:

'The finest and the happiest and carefree bunch of touring soccer players ever to hit the city pulled into the Canadian Pacific station Friday night, singing and joshing each other like a burgeon of happy kids with their school bags thrown down in the basement and two months' holidays ahead of them.'[10]

In the evening the tourists were entertained at a charity Rugby game when Miss Starr was moved to say *''What I like about your Canadian rugby is that ballet dancing,' said Miss Starr, referring to the line shifting as the signals were called.'*[11]

The game on the following day at Carruthers Park saw the Islington Corinthians make a slow start going 0-1 down after seven minutes. Bradbury equalised just prior to the interval, before Johnny Sherwood scored one of the best goals ever seen in the stadium when he hit a shot on the volley from 25 yards out which flew into the roof of the net.

After the game the I.C.'s were taken to dinner at the McLaren Hotel and it is evident that the locals greatly enjoyed their company:

'Now we had Charlton Athletic players last summer...and they hardly opened their mouths....But the fellows Saturday night, they were a scream...and that show they put on around the old piano is something Sam. 'Scrim,' Harry Strange, Jimmy Wardrope, Jack Bailie and Dan Shepherd will never forget. For over two hours Jack Braithwaite,

Alec Buchanan, Johnny Sherwood (at the piano), Eddy Martin (the only married soul in the team), Cyril Longman, George Pearce, Johnny Miller and Ted Wingfield sang song, ditties and what have you.'[12]

Travelling east to Ontario the Islington Corinthians recorded a comfortable 6-2 victory at Fort William, with their performance delighting the crowd, before arriving in Toronto. In Toronto the I.C.'s faced Ulster United, the Eastern Canadian champions. The report of the game describes the tourists' performance:

'Of course, you can't compare Corinthians with other teams that have come out from the Old Land to display their wares. The amateurs are not polished, positional stylists. But they do play the game robustly and, with Ulster doing the same; it's not hard to understand why the tussle developed into one of the tidiest tussles seen around here in some time.'[13]

The I.C.'s raced into a 2-0 lead after just twenty minutes, which Ulster United soon pulled back to 2-2. It was left to the prolific Johnny Sherwood to seal victory when he headed the winner on 61 minutes. The tourists were made to suffer for their victory though, as no oranges or towels was provided for them in the dressing rooms! This was pure oversight however and the local newspapers again raved about what great people the tourists were:

'The touring players proved to be a grand bunch. We met them yesterday noon at the T. Eaton luncheon in their honour. They toured the big store and created quite a bit of fun (and a few sales) at the moccasin counter.

... By their own admission, they weren't up to form last night. The train ride from Fort William to here apparently wasn't any picnic and the boys got only two hours sleep.'[14]

The tour was fast approaching its conclusion and on 26th May 1938, the Islington Corinthians visited Niagara Falls on the border between Ontario, Canada and New York State. The tour party stood beneath the falls in the cave of the winds, looking through the cascading water into the wreckage of the honeymoon bridge. It was to be the last amazing spectacle that the tourists would experience on their journey.

The following morning, the Islington Corinthians arrived at Windsor station, in Montreal, Quebec and were met by the local Rotarians and the representatives from the Provincial Soccer Board, before being taken to breakfast at the Queen's Hotel.

The tourists were determined to put on a good show and win their last match, so they selected their strongest possible line up. The Provincial Soccer Board was also anxious to take advantage of the exhibition and announced that all local players could gain entrance free of charge at half time for educational purposes. In the event, the I.C.'s were able to bring their journey through six provinces of Canada to a triumphant conclusion with their biggest win:

Left: The city of Niagara Falls

Left: Niagara Falls

Right: Islington Corinthians ready for Niagara Falls

Left: Under Niagara Falls

MONTREAL 2 ISLINGTON CORINTHIANS 7

'Islington Corinthians completed their globe encircling tour by soundly whipping the pick of the Montreal teams, 7-2, at Molson Stadium last night. Showing more polish and better play then some of the Old Country professional teams which have visited Canada in recent years, the noted amateurs gave a superb exhibition and gave the Montreal players a lesson in the finer points of the dribbling code. From goal to centre there was class. Adepts at trapping and clever with their heads the tourists varied their play as occasion demanded. Generally they adopted a long passing game with long thrusts through to the Montreal end and just as quickly turned to a short passing game that was equally effective. Positional play was almost faultless.

Defensively Montreal was good, but the attack seldom got within striking distance of Longman. Bates, although beaten seven times, gave a good exhibition between the posts.

Johnny Sherwood stole the spotlight by scoring five of the Corinthians goals. Sherwood, who has an average of more than two goals for each match in which he has played, was quite in his element of the green sward at the Molson Stadium. Some of his drives were terrific and his second goal went clean through the net despite, the fact that Bates got his hands to the ball ad slightly retarded its speed.

Dick Shorrock secured both of Montreal's goals, scoring the first from a penalty and heading in the second.

Montreal got off to a good start when Manning and Clark sandwiched Shorrock as he was dashing for the Corinthian goal. Referee Irving promptly awarded a penalty and Shorrock in turn converted it.

This was 12 minutes after the commencement and while Montreal continued to play well at the 29 minute mark Whittaker threaded the ball through to Sherwood who fired

Above: Signed team photo of the Islington Corinthians

in a shot that was labelled a goal all the way. Seven minutes later Sherwood was through again and this time his shot broke right through the goal net.

Four minutes from the end of the period a great save by Bates prevented Whittaker from scoring but with less than a minute to play Sherwood netted again. He headed three times and his final nod was into the net.

Less than a minute after the restart Montreal's goal fell again, this time to Braithwaite. Shorrock revived the Montreal hopes when he took Donald McLean's pass to head in a fine goal. Seven minutes later Sherwood took J. Miller's pass to head in the fifth goal for the visitors. At this stage Corinthians were almost completely in control. Sherwood got through again and fired point blank at Bates but the Montrealer cleared, but the impact was so great that he had to receive attention. Shortly afterwards Sherwood dribbled through again to fire in another goal. Ten minutes from the end Read caught the rebound when Sherwood struck the crossbar and Bates's charge fell again.'[15]

The tour was now at an end, and on 28th May 1938, the tourists set sail on the Empress of Australia from Quebec for Southampton, where they arrived on 5th June. By completing their journey the Islington Corinthians became the first team to circle the globe and were met on the docks by Mr Pickford, Mr Huband, Mr. Billy Heard and Stanley Rous. Mr Pickford led the congratulations:

'Many of us wondered whether you would have the pluck to go through with your ambitious project, unique in the history of the game.

We are proud of you, for you have literally kicked a football round the world. We thank you for putting football on the map.'[16]

The team had fostered empire relations as British ambassadors, travelling 35,000 miles and making football history. The team had played in thirteen different lands and played a grand total of 95 games in just eight months. Their record was extraordinary and their final tally of 65 victories and only eight defeats was an achievement that every member of the tour party could be proud of.

It was reported on their return that the club had lost £750 on their venture and Smith explained that *'undreamed of expenses ate into the profits.'*[17] The report stated however, that this sum was likely to be reimbursed by the Football Association by way of a belated grant. As a result the mission was accomplished and Smith had been justified in his theory that the club could pay their way around the world. Other revelations on their return were that one unnamed player had lost his job while he was away and that the team, despite a strenuous exercise programme, had put on an average of seven pounds in weight during the course of their tour! It was now time for the management and players to return to the real world and adjust to the nine to five routine which would soon be confronting them. They would, though, have a wealth of stories and wonderful memories to help dispel the inevitable sense of anticlimax.

CHAPTER ELEVEN

THE END

After such a successful tour it was perhaps inevitable that the club would struggle to emulate their previous success. The day to day grind of domestic matches would have been less appealing than in the early days of the club, and the Tufnell Park enclosure was out of action in any case. In the circumstances a lengthy fixture list was impractical and it is quite conceivable that Tom Smith would have preferred at this stage a Middlesex Wanderers style existence, which entailed touring and the occasional appearance in England.

Tom Smith was interviewed in late August 1938 and gave the following details of the club's immediate plans:

'Discussing the club's future plans with a GAZETTE representative. Mr. Tom Smith, the energetic secretary, intimated that regular mid-week matches had been dropped and the Corinthians were only going to play three or four matches with outside teams during the coming season. They would be special games, and one was expected to be with Spurs, though nothing had been fixed yet. There was a movement afoot to find a central headquarters for the club.'[1]

Smith said also that it was hoped in the future to plan a series of 'goodwill tours' involving travel to as many football playing countries as possible. He revealed that the Islington Corinthians had already received an invitation from Curacao (South America) and were considering a big South American tour in 1940. There is however little evidence to show that the club made progress in finding a central headquarters, and the war would undoubtedly have prevented construction of a stadium even if a site had been secured.

The next big event in the club's history was the World Tour Celebration Dinner which was held at Beale's Restaurant in Holloway on 4th October 1938. In attendance was an all-star cast of dignitaries and football guests which included Lt. Commander Tufnell, M.P. (President of the Club), the Mayor of Islington (Coun. Mrs. J.L. Blythe, J.P.), Mr

S.F. Rous (Secretary of the F.A.), Mr W.W. Heard (Secretary of the Middlesex F.A.), Mr Claude Dudley (President of Islington Rotary Club), Mr. J. Peart (Fulham F.C.) and Mr C.F.S. Slight. Present also were 16 of the 18 players who took part in the world tour.

Amidst the welter of congratulatory back slapping which these events generally tended to be, there followed a number of speeches. Mr. Dudley began by toasting 'The Club' and said they *'had done a power of good.'* He spoke also of the pride that Islington Rotary Club had in sponsoring the venture.

Tom Smith was next, emphasising his pride in the players who took part:

'Referring to the players he said. 'If I had had the whole of the amateurs in England to choose from I am confident that I could not have got a better team. I don't think any club has been asked to play 95 games in one season as we did. The boys really did put themselves out to accomplish what we intended and that was to increase abroad the prestige of English football.

They played as many clubs as they possibly could and whatever the race or colour of their opponents the players fraternised with them on and off the field.' [2]

Mr. Pickford representing the Football Association then added his congratulations - an ironic twist considering their grave doubts when the tour was originally proposed at the tail end of 1936:

'On behalf of the F.A. I would like to thank you for having made this tour because it is one of our great aims to endeavour to get one set of laws for Association Football all over the world, and by your example wherever you went you helped us to do this. You had no difficulty in playing the game as it should be played, and you maintained those traditions of good sportsmanship and fair play that are characteristic of our race.' [3]

The Mayor of Islington spoke next and concluded his remarks with an apology:

'I wonder whether the Corinthians have quite forgiven me for not welcoming them to the Town Hall when they returned. It was entirely due to the fact that I did not know the date of their return. I should have done so but I have so many things to remember that it is very easy to miss some things. I have not forgiven some people who could have jogged my memory about the Corinthians. I should have been only too pleased to have welcomed them back because I am proud of them and pleased to think that they went round the world not only as Englishmen but also as Islingtonians who have brought honour to the Borough.' [4]

Mr. Rous (later Sir Stanley) rounded off the speeches when he said if there was 'A Nobel prize' for Club managers Mr. Tom Smith well deserved it!

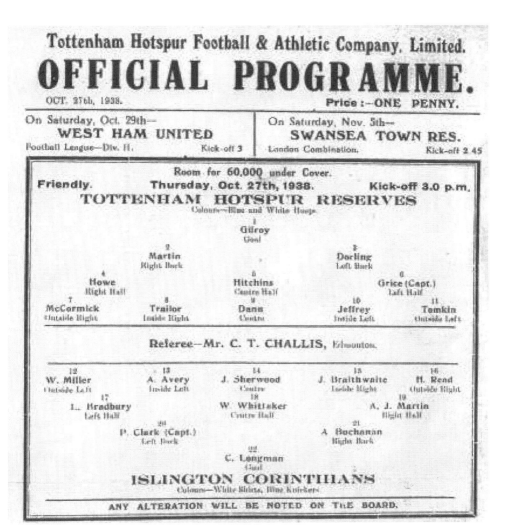

Above: Programme for Islington Corinthians v Tottenham Hotspur

Lt. Commander Tufnell handed out special badges and banners to the players present as mementoes of the tour, before the guests partied the night away with entertainment provided by Miss Loraine Peart , the star of 'Maritza' and the 'Street Musician,' together with Braithwaite's Band who provided the music for the dance.

1938/39

Tom Smith was true to his word about the Islington Corinthians' limited schedule for what turned out to be their final season. The problems with the Tufnell Park enclosure meant that only two games are known to have been played, both away.

181

Left: The Islington Corinthians
visit a sports shop on their
return in 1938

Courtesy of Islington Museum

Just three weeks after the celebration dinner, the Islington Corinthians played Tottenham Hotspur at White Hart Lane. An exciting 4-4 draw ensued with the team containing seven of the touring squad and one player, Nottage, who had featured for the I.C.'s for many years. The team that day was:

C. Longman, A.D. Buchanan, P. Clark, R. Cater, E. Martin, G. Hicks, J. Braithwaite, A. Goodman, J. Sherwood, H. Nottage, W. Miller.

The last known game that the Islington Corinthians played was on 30th November 1938 against the Royal Air Force, and was reported in *The Times* as follows:

R.A.F. 1   ISLINGTON CORINTHIANS 2

'The Royal Air Force had the better of the play in their game against Islington Corinthians at Uxbridge yesterday, but in the closing minutes A.H. Woolcock badly misjudged a dropping shot from H. Nottage, and the Islington Corinthians won by two goals to one.

That the R.A.F. did not at least save the game was largely due to weak finishing by their forwards. Indeed, D.O. Finlay seemed to be the only forward on the side capable of sending in a telling shot. Finlay seems to improve with every game he plays. His speed, which A.H. Gibbons exploited to the full, was, of course, a tremendous asset to his side's attack and the combination between these two players was a constant menace to the Islington Corinthians' defence.

The main strength of the Islington Corinthians lay in their half-back line, which was essentially constructive, but it was not until R.M. Tarrant moved back from centre-forward to one of the inside forward positions that the link between the half-backs and the front line of the attack was firmly established. Then the attack began to move forward with a smoothness and certainty which gave N. Gibson ample opportunity to show what a fine defensive player he is.

DEFENCE IN TROUBLE

Finlay and Gibbons soon had the Islington Corinthians' defence in trouble and Finlay sent in two shots which E. Ditchburn did well to save. When next Finlay broke away the goalkeeper was at fault, but P. Codd just managed to clear the final shot sent in by H.S. Genner. Rain now began to fall heavily and the foothold became more and more insecure. The R.A.F. passes began to lose some of their former accuracy. To add to the difficulties the ball sometimes either stopped almost dead after it had bounced or skidded along at an alarming pace. The R.A.F., however, quickly adapted themselves to the altered conditions and it was not long before Finlay picked up a through pass, beat the defence for speed, and sent in a shot, which gave Ditchburn no chance.

In the second half Gibbons, probably with the hope of adding to the thrust of the R.A.F. attack, occasionally changed places with his centre-forward. But, whatever the reason, it was certainly open to question, for he was far better employed constructing his side's attack in mid-field than he was waiting vainly for the final phases of an attack which seldom, if ever, came to anything. The Islington Corinthians, relieved of some of the pressure, began to open up the game, and in due course Tarrant ran forward to turn a centre from his right wing past Woolcock. Then came Woolcock's one and only mistake, and although the R.A.F. began again to show signs of their proper form the recovery came too late to be of much use.

Team:
E. Ditchburn, P. Codd, R. Mardn, L.C. Bradbury, S. Lown, G.J. Whittaker, H. Read, G. Jay, R.M. Tarrant, H. Nottage, A. Reeves'[5]

On this occasion, Smith could field only three of the tour party in Bradbury, Read and Tarrant. However, in goal was Ted Ditchburn (who after the war represented England in Full Internationals) from Tottenham's nursery team of Northfleet. There is very little mention of the Islington Corinthians from this point and they just disappeared from view.

South American & West Indies Tour 1940

The last references to the club concern the proposed tour of South America and the West Indies, which was due to take place in 1940. *'The Gleaner,'* Jamaica's leading newspaper, announced in September 1938 that Tom Smith had made contact with the Jamaican Football Association with a view to visiting the island. The proposal met with an enthusiastic response, but by this time the world's attention was focussed on the forthcoming war which now looked inevitable.

Fifteen months passed with no further news and *'The Gleaner'* then reported:

'WAR CALLS OFF PROPOSED TOUR OF CORINTHIANS

A news item appearing in one of last week's issues of the 'Gleaner' revealed the fact that the Islington Corinthians, famous for their world's football tour in 1938, have called off the proposed one of the West Indies and South America.

It will be remembered that at the last annual general meeting of the Jamaica Football Association the president read a letter from the English touring club which suggested that they stop off in Jamaica and play a series of matches during the cancelled tour.

As far as could be seen, whether war or not, the Islington's visit was the only one on view, and as the last international series were played in 1938, there is no doubt that it would be looked forward to with much interest.

There would be no hanky-panky about this tour. I can inform local players and adherents. The Corinthians can play football, as indicated, not only by the number of matches they won out of ninety odd games on their world's tour, but included among the larger proportion of their victories are those over full strength teams of South Africa and Australia (sic), which two countries produce the best players of the Empire outside of Great Britain.'[6]

What happened to the Islington Corinthians?

The question of what happened to the Islington Corinthians is matter of conjecture. The initial problem was the issue of the Tufnell Park enclosure. This was unavailable for the 1938/39 season so Islington Corinthians' co-tenants London Caledonians played at Barking. Tufnell Park themselves used Park Royal F.C. and Golders Green in order to carry on. At the end of the season the London Caledonians effectively disbanded, although remaining registered with the F.A., citing playing and financial difficulties (no doubt exacerbated by the absence of 'home' games during the 1938/39 season). The Tufnell Park enclosure, however, was to be open again for 1939/40 season after the ground had been repaired and Tufnell Park F.C. were due to return home. The ground problems then resurfaced and Tufnell Park played during the war years at Golders Green F.C. (now known as Hendon F.C.), before relocating finally to Cheshunt after the conclusion of hostilities. It is strange that the owners of the Tufnell Park enclosure caused so many problems as it still exists in the form of a park, albeit without the stand which once stood on the Campdale Road side of the road, and has never been redeveloped.

World War Two was obviously a major problem for the Islington Corinthians. While they had been touring the world the Axis powers of Germany and Italy had grown bolder and in March 1938, Germany annexed Austria with little more than verbal protests by way of response from the other European powers. This only emboldened

Hitler and he next began making claims on behalf of those Germans living in the Sudetenland region of western Czechoslovakia. These areas were also ceded to him, on the understanding that he would make no further territorial demands. In March 1939, Hitler reneged on this agreement and effectively occupied all of Czechoslovakia (a puppet government being installed in Slovakia). The world began to take note and it was at this point that Britain and France guaranteed their military support for Polish independence, which was later extended to Romania and Greece. As a result of this pact, when Hitler invaded Poland in September 1939 and refused to withdraw, Britain and France declared war on Germany.

The war meant that the Islington Corinthians would struggle to survive both because of a shortage of players and the absence of a ground. It was ironic as perhaps this was when they could have been at their most useful, raising funds for the many needy causes arising from the war.

Another question concerns Tom Smith and his reasons for letting the club disappear when he might have been expected to build on its growing celebrity. It was after all his baby; he had founded the club and been its inspiration since day one and without him they would never have had the ambition to undertake such a momentous voyage.

The name Tom Smith as researchers will appreciate is not necessarily the easiest to pursue, but clues do exist as to his later years. It is unlikely that he perished in any of the German bombing raids, as his business premises at 57 Compton Road, Islington were still listed in the 1944 Post Office Business Directory, although they disappear a year later. This property is still in existence and occupies the basement area of one of the buildings in Compton Road. His home (when he was a councillor in the 1930's) also survives at 138 Pinner Road, Harrow. This is now the offices of Stephen Daniel & Co., a firm of Chartered Accountants, so it is unlikely that anything untoward happened to him as a result of the war.

It seems much more likely that he reached retirement age and simply closed the business. Tom Smith had helped found the Old Hanoverians in 1902, which suggests he would have been born in the early 1880's, and thus by 1944 he would have been approaching the male retirement age of 65 set in 1940 and ready to call it a day. For someone who was as active as Tom Smith it is strange that he would just retire and give up his lifelong obsession with football, but what is clear is that the Islington Corinthians were never destined to re-emerge after the war. Smith would no doubt have lost many of the contacts which enabled him to field such a competitive side for the world tour and retirements from the game, loss of life and the fact that amateur football was dramatically scaled down during the war all weighed heavily against any scheme to revive the club.

Whatever the reason for the club's untimely end, which we will surely never know for certain, Tom Smith and his Islington Corinthians deserve to be remembered for their contribution to the global game, not to mention their record-breaking itinerary. It is highly unlikely that such an ambitious project will ever be undertaken again, unless a Russian billionaire steps in and creates football's equivalent of the Harlem Globetrotters. Even an amateur or semi-professional club side could not now contemplate undertaking such a trip, as it would involve sacrifices that few players would be in a position to accept. Above all the time has long gone when English football set the standard to which other nations aspired and a team of amateurs, however Corinthian in spirit, would make very little impression on the hearts and minds of those accustomed to satellite coverage of the very best of the sport from around the world.

ISLINGTON CORINTHIANS WORLD TOUR
RESULTS AND STATISTICS

5th October 1937
Rotterdam
VUC 0 Islington Corinthians 0 attendance 3,000
Team: Unknown

6th October 1937
Amsterdam
Haarlem 0 Islington Corinthians 2
Scorers: Sherwood, Miller
Team: Unknown

7th October 1937
Amsterdam
Amsterdam DWV 1 Islington Corinthians 1
Scorer: Tarrant
Team: Unknown

10th October 1937
Zurich
Winterthur 0 Islington Corinthians 3
Scorers: Unknown
Team: Unknown

12th October 1937
Berne
Berne 1 Islington Corinthians 4
Scorers: Unknown
Team: Unknown

22nd October 1937
Cairo
Cairo XI 1 Islington Corinthians 1 attendance 4,000
Scorer: Miller J.W.
Team: Longman C., Manning R.L., Clark P.B., Dance G.W., Whittaker W., Wright J.K., Read
H.C., Bradbury L., Tarrant R.P., Avery A., Miller J.W.

24th October 1937
Alexandria
Alexandria 1 Islington Corinthians 2 attendance 5,000
Scorers: Sherwood, Miller J.W.
Team: Longman C., Manning R.L., Clark P.B., Dance G.W., Whittaker W., Wright J.K., Read
H.C., Bradbury L. Tarrant R.P., Sherwood J., Pearce G.W. (Miller J.W.)

29th October 1937
Cairo
Cairo XI 1 Islington Corinthians 2 attendance 2,500
Scorers: Read, Miller W.
Team: Longman C., Manning R.L. Clark P.B., Dance G.W., Whittaker W., Wright J.K., Read
H.C., Bradbury L., Tarrant R.P., Sherwood J. Miller W.

31st October 1937
Port Said
Canal Zone XI 4 Islington Corinthians 1 attendance 3,000
Scorer: Bradbury
Team: Longman C., Manning R.L. Clark P.B., Dance G.W., Whittaker W., Wright J.K., Read
H.C., Bradbury L., Avery A., Sherwood J., Miller W.

13th November 1937
Calcutta
Mohammedan Sporting Club 0 Islington Corinthians 0 attendance 50,000
Team: Longman C., Martin E., Clark P.B., Dance G.W., Whittaker W., Wright J.K., Read H.C.,
Bradbury L., Sherwood J., Avery A., Miller J.W.

14th November 1937
Jamshedpur
All Blues 2 Islington Corinthians 5
Scorers: Tarrant 2, Avery 2, Braithwaite
Team: Unknown

15th November 1937
Jamshedpur
All Blues 0 Islington Corinthians 1
Scorers: Unknown
Team: Unknown

16th November 1937
Calcutta
Mohon Bagun 0 Islington Corinthians 1 Attendance 40,000
Scorer: Tarrant
Team: Longman C., Martin E., Clark P.B., Miller W., Whittaker W., Wright J.K., Braithwaite
J.C., Bradbury L., Tarrant R.P., Avery A., Miller J.W.

17th November 1937
Calcutta
Indian F.A. XI 1 Islington Corinthians 1 attendance 50,000
Scorer: Bradbury
Team: Longman C., Martin E., Clark P.B., Wright J.K., Whittaker W., Miller W., Read H.C.,
Bradbury L., Tarrant R.P., Miller J.W., Pearce G.W.

20th November 1937
Calcutta
All India XI 0 Islington Corinthians 2 attendance 55,000
Scorers: Clark, Tarrant
Team: Longman C., Martin E., Clark P.B., Wright J.K., Whittaker W., Miller W., Read H.C., Bradbury L., Tarrant R.P., Avery A., Miller J.W.

21st November 1937
Dacca
Dacca Sporting Association 1 Islington Corinthians 0
Team: Wingfield T., Manning R.L., Buchanan A.D., Dance D.W., Whittaker W., Miller W., Braithwaite J.C., Avery A., Tarrant R.P., Sherwood J., Miller J.W.

22nd November 1937
Dacca
Dacca Sporting Association 0 Islington Corinthians 1
Scorer: Tarrant
Team: Longman C., Martin E., Clark P.B., Dance G.W., Whittaker W., Wright J.K., Read H.C, Bradbury L., Tarrant R.P., Avery A., Miller J.W.

23rd November 1937
Mymensingh
Mymensingh 0 Islington Corinthians 6
Scorers: Tarrant 3, Sherwood 2, Read
Team: Longman C., Manning R.L., Buchanan A.D., Dance G.W, Whittaker W., Wright J.K., Sherwood J., Read H.C., Tarrant R.P., Miller W., Miller J.W.

24th November 1937
Kishoreganj
Kishoreganj XI 0 Islington Corinthians 3
Scorers: Tarrant, Sherwood 2
Team: Wingfield T., Manning R.L., Buchanan A.D., Bradbury L., Martin E., Miller W., Sherwood J., Tarrant R.P., Miller J.W., Avery A., Pearce G.W.

25th November 1937
Comilla
Combined Comilla XI 0 Islington Corinthians 3
Scorers: Sherwood, Read, Miller J.
Team: Longman C., Martin E., Clark P.B., Bradbury L., Whittaker W., Wright J.K., Sherwood J. Read H.C., Tarrant R.P., Miller W., Miller J.W.

26th November 1937
Chittagong
Chittagong 0 Islington Corinthians 1   attendance 77,000
Scorer: Sherwood
Team: Wingfield T., Manning R.L., Buchanan A.D., Bradbury L. Whittaker W., Wright J.K., Sherwood J., Read H.C., Tarrant R.P., Miller W., Pearce G.W.

27th November 1937
Rajshahi
1st Battalion Cameronians Rifles 0 Islington Corinthians 2
Scorers: Unknown
Team: Unknown

30th November 1937
Berhampore
Wheeler Memorial Shield XI 1 Islington Corinthians 3 attendance 4,000
Scorers: Braithwaite, Read, Miller J.
Team: Longman C., Manning R.L., Clark P.B., Bradbury L., Whittaker W., Wright J.K., Sherwood J., Read H.C., Braithwaite J.C., Miller W., Pearce G.W.

2nd December 1937
Baripada
Mayurbhanj Athletic Association 0 Islington Corinthians 1   attendance 3,000
Scorer: Braithwaite
Team: Wingfield T., Manning R.L., Buchanan A.D., Dance G.W., Whittaker W., Wright J.K., Sherwood J., Avery A., Braithwaite J.C., Miller W., Pearce G.W.

3rd December 1937
Kharagpur
Bengal Nagpur Railway 1 Islington Corinthians 3
Scorer: Tarrant 2, Bradbury
Team: Longman C., Manning R.L., Clark P.B., Bradbury L., Whittaker W., Wright J.K., Sherwood J., Read H.C., Tarrant R.P., Miller W., Miller J.W.

5th December 1937
Hazaribagh
Indian F.A. XI 0 Islington Corinthians 1
Scorer: Avery
Team: Longman C., Manning R.L., Clark P.B., Bradbury L., Whittaker W., Wright J.K., Sherwood J., Avery A., Braithwaite J.C., Miller W., Miller J.W.

6th December 1937
Dhanbad
All-India XI 0 Islington Corinthians 0
Team: Wingfield T., Clark P.B., Buchanan A.D., Bradbury L., Whittaker W., Wright J.K., Read H.C., Sherwood J., Braithwaite J.C., Avery A., Miller J.W.

7th December 1937
Jamalpur
Jamalpur 1 Islington Corinthians 2   attendance 3,000
Scorers: Tarrant, Bradbury
Team: Unknown

8th December 1937
Patna
Bihir 0 Islington Corinthians 5
Scorers: Unknown
Team: Unknown

10th December 1937
Lucknow
Lucknow Brigade 1 Islington Corinthians 4
Scorers: Miller J., Tarrant, Read, 1 unknown
Team: Longman C., Manning R.L., Clark P.B., Dance G.W., Whittaker W., Wright J.K., Read H.C., Bradbury L., Tarrant R.P., Avery A., Miller J.W.

11th December 1937
Lucknow
United Province XI 0 Islington Corinthians 0
Team: Wingfield T., Manning R.L., Buchanan A.D., Bradbury L., Whittaker W., Dance G.W., Braithwaite J.C., Sherwood J., Tarrant R.P., Miller W., Miller J.W.

13th December 1937
Delhi
Delhi 0 Islington Corinthians 2
Scorers: Read, Tarrant
Team: Wingfield T., Buchanan A.D., Clark P.B., Dance G.W., Martin E., Wright J.K., Read H.C., Bradbury L., Tarrant R.P., Miller W., Sherwood J.

14th December 1937
Ajmer
Ajmer Association XI 1 Islington Corinthians 3
Scorers: Manning, Pearce, Sherwood
Team: Unknown

16th December 1937
Delhi
Young Men's Club 0 Islington Corinthians 1   attendance 1,000
Scorer: Sherwood
Team: Longman C., Manning R.L., Buchanan A.D., Bradbury L., Whittaker W., Wright J.K., Read H.C., Sherwood J., Braithwaite J.C., Miller W., Pearce G.W.E.

18th December 1937
Peshawar
Northwest Frontier 0 Islington Corinthians 3
Scorers: Braithwaite, Tarrant, Read
Team: Wingfield T., Manning R.L., Buchanan A.D., Wright J.K., Whittaker W., Bradbury L., Read H.C., Braithwaite J.C., Tarrant R.P., Sherwood J., Miller W.

19th December 1937
Peshawar
Army & Airforce XI 1 Islington Corinthians 2
Scorers: Tarrant, Read
Team: Unknown

20th December 1937
Lahore
Northwest India F.A. 0 Islington Corinthians 0   attendance 7,000
Team: Wingfield T., Clark P.B., Buchanan A.D., Wright J.K., Whittaker W., Dance G.W., Miller W., Sherwood J. Tarrant R.P., Braithwaite J.C., Bradbury L.

22nd December 1937
Benares
Benares 1 Islington Corinthians 7
Scorers: Tarrant 3, Sherwood 2, Miller J. 2
Team: Unknown

24th December 1937
Hetampur
Indian F.A. 0 Islington Corinthians 2
Scorers: Tarrant, Miller W.
Team: Unknown

28th December 1937
Calcutta
All-Blues 0 Islington Corinthians 2
Scorers: Unknown
Team: Unknown

30th December 1937
Calcutta
King's Own Scottish Borderers 0 Islington Corinthians 2 attendance 2,000
Scorers: Tarrant 2
Team: Unknown

3rd January 1938
Rangoon
All-Burmese XI 1 Islington Corinthians 1 attendance 16,000
Scorers: Tarrant
Team: Unknown

5th January 1938
Rangoon
Burma 1 Islington Corinthians 0 attendance 16,000
Team: Unknown

11th January 1938
Penang
Penang Asiatics 1 Islington Corinthians 4
Scorers: Avery, Read, Sherwood 2
Team: Longman C., Manning R.L., Buchanan A.D, Wright J.K., Whittaker W., Bradbury L., Read H.C., Avery A., Tarrant R.P., Sherwood J., Miller J.W.

13th January 1938
Alor Star
Kedah State 0 Islington Corinthians 0
Team: Unknown

14th January 1938
Penang
All-Penang 1 Islington Corinthians 3
Scorers: Miller J., Read, Sherwood
Team: Wingfield T., Martin E., Buchanan A.D., Dance G.W, Whittaker W., Bradbury L., Read H.C., Tarrant R.P., Sherwood J, Avery A., Miller J.W.

16th January 1938
Perak
Perak F.A. 1 Islington Corinthians 3
Scorers: Sherwood 2, Miller J.
Team: Longman C., Manning R.L., Buchanan A.D., Dance G.W., Whittaker W., Bradbury L., Read H.C., Tarrant R.P., Sherwood J, Avery A., Miller J.W.

17th January 1938
Ipoh
Perak F.A. 0 Islington Corinthians 3
Scorers: Tarrant, Sherwood, Pearce
Team: Wingfield T., Manning R.L., Buchanan A.D., Martin E., Whittaker W., Bradbury L., Read H.C., Tarrant R.P., Sherwood J., Avery A., Pearce G.W.E.

18th January 1938
Seremban
Negri Sembilan XI 1 Islington Corinthians 4
Scorers: Sherwood, Bradbury, Pearce 2
Team: Longman C., Manning R.L., Buchanan A.D., Martin E., Whittaker W., Bradbury L., Braithwaite J.C., Tarrant R.P., Sherwood J., Avery A., Pearce G.W.E.

20th January 1938
Malacca
Malacca 1 Islington Corinthians 2
Scorers: Sherwood 2
Team: Wingfield T., Manning R.L., Buchanan A.D., Martin E., Whittaker W., Wright J.K., Braithwaite J.C., Miller W., Sherwood J., Avery A., Pearce G.W.E.

22nd January 1938
Kuala Lumpar
T.P.C.A. 1 Islington Corinthians 1
Scorer: Pearce
Team: Longman C., Manning R.L., Buchanan A.D., Martin E., Whittaker W., Bradbury L., Read H.C., Tarrant R.P., Sherwood J., Avery A., Pearce G.W.E.

24th January 1938
Kuala Lumpar
Selangor 0 Islington Corinthians 2   attendance 9,000
Scorers: Sherwood 2
Team: Wingfield T., Martin E., Buchanan A.D., Wright J.K., Whittaker W., Bradbury L., Read H.C., Tarrant R.P., Sherwood J., Avery A., Miller J.W.

26th January 1938
Singapore
Straights Chinese 0 Islington Corinthians 5   attendance 10,000
Scorers: Sherwood 5
Team: Longman C., Martin E., Buchanan A.D., Wright J.K., Whittaker W., Bradbury L., Read H.C., Tarrant R.P., Sherwood J., Avery A., Miller W.

30th January 1938
Singapore
All-Singapore 2 Islington Corinthians 3
Scorers: Avery 2, Sherwood
Team: Wingfield T., Martin E., Buchanan A.D., Wright J.K., Whittaker W., Bradbury L., Read H.C., Tarrant R.P., Sherwood J., Avery A., Miller W.

1st February 1938
Singapore
Combined Service 0 Islington Corinthians 1
Scorer: Sherwood
Team: Longman C., Martin E., Clark P.B., Wright J.K., Whittaker W., Bradbury L., Read H.C., Tarrant R.P., Sherwood J., Avery A., Miller W.

2nd February 1938
Singapore
S.A.F.C. XI 1 Islington Corinthians 4
Scorers: Avery, Sherwood 2, Bradbury
Team: Longman C., Manning R.L., Buchanan A.D., Wright J.K., Whittaker W., Bradbury L., Read H.C, Tarrant R.P., Sherwood J., Avery A., Miller W.

4th February 1938
Malacca
Malacca 0 Islington Corinthians 6
Scorers: Bradbury 2, Tarrant 2, Avery, Braithwaite
Team: Longman C., Martin E., Buchanan A.D., Wright J.K., Whittaker W., Bradbury L.C., Read H.C., Braithwaite J.C., Tarrant R.P., Avery A., Miller J.W.

6th February 1938
Singapore
All-Malaya 0 Islington Corinthians 3   attendance 15,000
Scorers: Avery, Tarrant, Braithwaite
Team: Longman C., Martin E., Buchanan A.D., Wright J.K., Whittaker W., Bradbury L., Read
H.C., Braithwaite J.C., Tarrant R.P., Avery A., Miller J.W.

8th February 1938
Batu Pahat
Johore 1 Islington Corinthians 7
Scorers: Miller W. 3, Avery 2, Manning, Martin
Team: Longman C., Martin E., Clark P.B., Dance G.W., Whittaker W., Wright J.K., Manning
R.L., Braithwaite J.C., Miller W., Avery A., Pearce G.W.E.

11th February 1938
Saigon
Saigon Selected XI 0 Islington Corinthians 0
Team: Unknown

12th February 1938
Saigon
Saigon Selected XI 2 Islington Corinthians 5
Scorers: Tarrant 4, Avery
Team: Unknown

13th February 1938
Saigon
All-Cochin China XI 0 Islington Corinthians 1
Scorer: Avery
Team: Unknown

19th February 1938
Hong Kong
South China A.A. 0 Islington Corinthians 1
Scorer: Avery
Team: Longman C., Clark P.B., Buchanan A.D., Martin E., Whittaker W., Wright J.K.,
Manning R.L., Bradbury L. Tarrant R.P. Avery A., Miller ?

20th February 1938
Hong Kong
Combined Services 1 Islington Corinthians 3
Scorers: Bradbury, Tarrant, Pearce
Team: Wingfield T., Clark P.B., Buchanan A.D., Dance G.W., Whittaker W., Wright J.K.,
Bradbury L., Miller W., Tarrant R.P., Avery A., Pearce G.W.E.

26th February 1938
Hong Kong
Civilians 1 Islington Corinthians 3
Scorers: Sherwood 3
Team: Wingfield T., Martin E., Clark P.B., Wright J.K., Whittaker W., Bradbury L., Read H.C., Tarrant R.P., Sherwood J., Avery A., Pearce G.W.E.

27th February 1938
Hong Kong
All-Hong Kong 1 Islington Corinthians 5
Scorers: Sherwood 2, Avery 2, Read
Team: Longman C., Martin E., Clark P.B., Wright J.K., Whittaker W., Bradbury L., Read H.C., Tarrant R.P., Sherwood J., Avery A., Pearce G.W.E.

28th February 1938
Macao
Selected XI Macao 1 Islington Corinthians 1   attendance 3,000
Scorers: Manning
Team: Longman C., Clark P.B., Buchanan A.D., Dance G.W., Whittaker W., Wright J.K., Manning R.L., Bradbury L., Miller W., Pearce G.W.E., Miller J.W.

2nd March 1938
Hong Kong
Combined Police & Club XI 2 Islington Corinthians 4
Scorers: Read, Sherwood 2, Braithwaite
Team: Longman C. (Wingfield T.), Martin E., Buchanan A.D. (Manning R.L.), Wright J.K. (Clark P.B.), Whittaker W., Bradbury L. Read H.C. (Dance G.W.), Braithwaite J.C., Sherwood J., Miller W. (Avery A.), Miller J.W.

9th March 1938
Manila
Chinese XI 0 Islington Corinthians 9
Scorers: Unknown
Team: Unknown

11th March 1938
Manila
Santo Tomas University 0 Islington Corinthians 0
Team: Unknown

13th March 1938
Manila
University de la Salle 0 Islington Corinthians 0
Team: Unknown

16th March 1938
Manila
Y.C.O. Athletic Club 0 Islington Corinthians 2
Scorers: Unknown
Team: Unknown

18th March 1938
Manila
Letran College 1 Islington Corinthians 3
Scorers: Unknown
Team: Unknown

21st March 1938
Manila
All-Manila 3 Islington Corinthians 0
Team: Unknown

23rd March 1938
Manila
University de la Salle 1 Islington Corinthians 4
Scorers: Unknown
Team: Unknown

27th March 1938
Manila
All-Manila 1 Islington Corinthians 0
Team: Unknown

30th March 1938
Hong Kong
South China A.A. 1 Islington Corinthians 1
Scorer: Pearce
Team: Longman C., Clark P.B., Buchanan A.D., Wright J.K., Whittaker W., Bradbury L., Read H.C., Tarrant R.P., Sherwood J., Miller ?. Pearce G.W.E.

31st March 1938
Hong Kong
South China & Navy XI 0 Islington Corinthians 2
Scorers: Miller J., Bickford
Team: Longman C., Manning R.L., Strange *, Dance G.W., Forrow *, Brittain *. Lamb *, Braithwaite J.C., Foweir *, Miller J.W., Bickford *
* Guest players

The above match was an unofficial game, but is recorded here for the record.

3rd April 1938
Shanghai
Shanghai All-Stars 3 Islington Corinthians 0   attendance 10,000
Team: Longman C., Martin E., Clark P.B., Wright J.K., Whittaker W., Bradbury L., Read H.C., Braithwaite J.C., Sherwood J., Tarrant R.P., Miller ?

7th April 1938
Tokyo
All-Kwanto 4 Islington Corinthians 0   attendance 50,000
Team: Longman C., Martin E., Clark P.B., Wright J.K., Whittaker W., Bradbury L., Pearce
G.W.E., Read H.C., Braithwaite J.C., Tarrant R.P., Miller ?

15th April 1938
Honolulu
Oahu All-Stars 0 Islington Corinthians 10
Scorers: Read 4, Sherwood 2, Bradbury 2, Miller J. 2
Team: Wingfield T., Manning R.L., Clark P.B., Wright J.K., Whittaker W., Martin E., Read
H.C., Bradbury L., Sherwood J., Miller W., Miller J.W.

24th April 1938
Los Angeles
Douglas Aircraft 0 Islington Corinthians 0
Team: Longman C., Manning R.L., Clark P.B., Wright J.K., Whittaker W., Martin E., Read
H.C., Bradbury L., Sherwood J., Miller W., Miller J.W.

26th April 1938
Los Angeles
All-Stars 1 Islington Corinthians 4   attendance 6,000
Scorers: Sherwood 2, Martin, Braithwaite
Team: Unknown

1st May 1938
San Francisco
North Californian All-Stars 2 Islington Corinthians 3
Scorers: Miller W., Tarrant, Miller J.
Team: Unknown

4th May 1938
San Francisco
North Californian All-Stars 2 Islington Corinthians 2
Scorers: Sherwood, Braithwaite
Team: Unknown

7th May 1938
Vancouver
Mainland All-Stars 2 Islington Corinthians 2   attendance 5,000
Scorers: Miller J., Tarrant
Team: Longman C., Martin E., Clark P.B., Wright J.K., Whittaker W., Bradbury L., Braithwaite
J.C., Sherwood J., Tarrant R.P., Miller W., Miller J.W.

9th May 1938
Naniamo
Naniamo 3 Islington Corinthians 2   attendance 1,500
Scorers: Sherwood 2
Team: Longman C., Manning R.L., Clark P.B., Dance G.W., Whittaker W., Martin E., Read
H.C., Sherwood J., Tarrant R.P., Miller W., Miller J.W.

11th May 1938
Victoria
Victoria 3 Islington Corinthians 6 attendance 1,624
Scorers: Tarrant 2, Miller J., OG, Sherwood 2
Team: Wingfield T., Buchanan A.D., Clark P.B., Wright J.K., Whittaker W., Bradbury L.,
Braithwaite J.C., Sherwood J., Tarrant R.P., Miller W., Miller J.W.

12th May 1938
Vancouver
Mainland All-Stars 3 Islington Corinthians 0   attendance 3,718
Team: Longman C., Buchanan A.D., Clark P.B., Wright J.K., Whittaker W., Martin E.,
Braithwaite J.C., Bradbury L., Sherwood J., Miller W., Miller J.W.

14th May 1938
Calgary
Calgary 0 Islington Corinthians 3   attendance 2,500
Scorers: Braithwaite 2, Sherwood
Team: Wingfield T., Buchanan A.D., Manning R.L., Dance G.W., Martin E., Bradbury L., Read
H.C., Sherwood J., Braithwaite J.C., Miller W., Miller J.W.

16th May 1938
Lethbridge
Lethbridge 2 Islington Corinthians 4
Scorers: Bradbury 2, Reid, Braithwaite
Team: Longman C., Clark P.B., Manning R.L., Martin E., Whittaker W., Wright J.K., Bradbury
L., Miller J.W., Sherwood J., Read H.C., Braithwaite J.C. SUB Pearce G.W.E.

18th May 1938
Saskatoon
Saskatoon 0 Islington Corinthians 3   attendance 1,500
Scorers: Read, Bradbury 2
Team: Longman C., Manning R.L., Clark P.B., Wright J.K., Whittaker W., Dance G.W.,
Braithwaite J.C., Read H.C., Bradbury L., Miller W., Miller J.W.

19th May 1938
Regina
Regina 0 Islington Corinthians 3   attendance 1,500
Scorers: Sherwood, Braithwaite, Bradbury
Team: Wingfield T., Manning R.L., Martin E., Wright J.K., Whittaker W., Miller W., Read
H.C., Braithwaite J.C., Bradbury L., Sherwood J., Pearce G.W.E.

21st May 1938
Winnipeg
Manitoba 1 Islington Corinthians 2   attendance 2,500
Scorers: Bradbury, Sherwood
Team: Longman C., Manning R.L., Clark P.B., Martin E., Whittaker W., Wright J.K.,
Braithwaite J.C., Bradbury L. Sherwood J., Miller W., Miller J.W.

23rd May 1938
Fort William
Fort William 2 Islington Corinthians 6 attendance 700
Scorers: Pearce, Sherwood 2, Miller J. 2, Braithwaite
Team: Wingfield T., Buchanan A.D., Clark P.B., Dance G.W., Whittaker W., Martin E., Read
H.C., Braithwaite J.C., Sherwood J., Pearce G.W.E., Miller J.W.

25th May 1938
Toronto
Ulster United 2 Islington Corinthians 3 attendance 1,500
Scorers: Miller J. 2, Sherwood
Team: Longman C., Manning R.L., Clark P.B., Wright J.K., Whittaker W., Dance G.W.,
Braithwaite J.C., Sherwood J., Bradbury L., Miller W., Miller J.W.

27th May 1938
Montreal
Montreal 2 Islington Corinthians 7
Scorers: Sherwood 5, Braithwaite, Miller J.
Team: Longman C., Manning R.L., Clark P.B., Bradbury L., Whittaker W., Dance G.W., Read
H.C., Braithwaite J.C., Sherwood J., Miller W., Miller J.W.

Note: The Islington Corinthians played 96 games, plus one unofficial match as listed above. There are discrepancies with the list of results published by the I.C.'s, however the statistics listed here are correct as per the authors investigations. The title of the book derives from the I.C.'s claims of playing 95 games.

BIBLIOGRAPHY

Books
Alaway, R., *Football All Around the World* (Newservice Ltd, 1948)
Badger, A.J., *The New Deal, The Depression Years 1933-1940* (MacMillan Education Ltd, 1989)
De Schweinitz, Jr, K., *The Rise & Fall of British India* (J.W. Arrowsmith Ltd., 1983)
Edwards, M., *British India 1772-1947* (Sidgwick & Johnson, 1967)
Flower, R., *Napoleon to Nasser* (Compton Press, 1972)
Gernet, J., *A History of Chinese Civilization* (Cambridge University Press, 1996)
Geyl, P., *The history of the Low Countries* (MacMillan & Co. Ltd, 1964)
Jahan, R., *Bangladesh Promise & Performance* (Zed Books Ltd, 2000)
Karnow, S., *Vietnam, A History* (Pimlico, 1994)
Ruane, K., *War & Revolution in Vietnam 1930-1975* (UCL Press, 1998)
Ryan, N.J., *The making of modern Malaysia & Singapore* (Oxford University Press, 1972)
Storry, R., *A History of Modern Japan* (Penguin Books, 1960)
Traynor, J., *Mastering Modern United States History* (Palgrave, 2001)
Von der Mehden, *South East Asia 1930-1970* (Thames & Hudson, 1974)
Wernstedt & Spencer, *The Philippine Island World* (Cambridge University Press, 1967)
Young, Bussink, Hasan, *Malaysia Growth & Equality in a multiracial society* (John Hopkins University Press, 1980)

Newspapers & Magazines
China Press, Clacton Times, Egyptian Gazette, Gazette (The), Gleaner (The), Globe & Mail, Honolulu Star Bulletin, Islington Gazette. Japan Weekly Chronicle, Lethbridge Herald, Los Angeles Times, Malayan Tribune, News Chronicle, San Francisco Chronicle, Scotsman (The), South China Morning Press, Star of India, Surrey Comet, Times (The), Times of India, Tunbridge Wells Advertiser, Winnipeg Free Press, World Sports

Websites
archive.mehstg.com
www.bangladesherkhela.com
www.margatefchistory.co.uk
www.newsflash.org
www.rsssf.com
www.sacu.org
victorian.fortunecity.com

Television
The World At War

Thanks
Sian Murphy
Phillips Brothers
Colin Walton
Dave Farebrother
John Laurence
Ray Armfield
Allard Doesburg
Islington Local History Centre
Colindale Newspaper Library
British Library, Book Depository
Colin Jose
Peter Jones
Thelma Cavallini
Mick Magic
Steve Menary
Alison Lister
Matthew Holland

REFERENCES

Chapter One
1 *Islington Gazette* 8.6.32 p1
2 *Islington Gazette* 24.3.1936 p1
3 *Islington Gazette* 9.9.1932 p1
4 *Islington Gazette* 8.2.1933 p1
5 *Islington Gazette* 22.3.1933 p1
6 *Islington Gazette* 22.3.1933 p1
7 *Islington Gazette* 17.3.1933 p1
8 *Islington Gazette* 16.8.1933 p2
9 *Islington Gazette* 28.7.1933 p2
10 *Islington Gazette* 13.9.1933 p1
11 *Islington Gazette* 26.9.1933 p1
12 *Islington Gazette* 17.10.1933 p3
13 *Islington Gazette* 9.2.1934 p3
14 *Islington Gazette* 21.2.1934 p2
15 *Islington Gazette* 16.11.1934 p1
16 *Islington Gazette* 3.5.1935 p2
17 *Islington Gazette* 5.6.1935 p1
18 *Islington Gazette* 15.11.1935 p2
19 *Islington Gazette* 31.12.1935 p2
20 *Islington Gazette* 24.3.1936 p1

Chapter Two
1 *Islington Gazette* 21.8.1936 p5
2 *News Chronicle* 1.9.1936 p12
3 *South China Morning Press* 25.2.1938 p8
4 *Islington Gazette* 23.12.1936 p2
5 *Malayan Tribune (Singapore)* 3.2.1938 p13
6 *South China Morning Press* 25.2.1938 p8
7 *Islington Gazette* 28.4.1937 p2
8 *Islington Gazette* 7.10.1938 p3
9 *Malayan Tribune (Singapore)* 10.1.1938 p14
10 *Islington Gazette* 10.9.1937 p1
11 *Islington Gazette* 10.9.1937 p1
12 *Islington Gazette* 7.10.1938 p3
13 *Islington Gazette* 10.9.1937 p1

Chapter Three
1 *Alaway* – Football All Around the World p 98
2 *Surrey Comet* 21.8.1937 p5
3 *Clacton Times* 2.10.1937 p2
4 *Tunbridge Wells Advertiser* 13.8.1937 p2
5 *Surrey Comet* 21.81937 p5

Chapter Four
1 *Alaway* Football All Around the World p 97
2 *Alaway* Football All Around the World p 98
3 *Geyl* The history of the Low Countries p215
4 *Malayan Tribune (Singapore)* 10.1.1938 p14
5 *Times of India* 12.11.1937 p17
6 *Malayan Tribune* 3.2.1938 p13
7 *Alaway* Football All Around the World p 99-100
8 *Alaway* Football All Around the World p100
9 *Flower* Napoleon to Nasser p150
10 *Egyptian Gazette* 21.10.1937 p2
11 *Islington Gazette* 24.6.1938 p5
12 *Alaway* Football All Around the World p100
13 *Egyptian Gazette* 23.10.1937 p4
14 *Egyptian Gazette* 25.10.1937 p2
15 *Egyptian Gazette* 3.11.1937 p2
16 *Egyptian Gazzette* 2.11.1937 p2
17 *Egyptian Gazette* 3.11.1937 p2
18 *Egyptian Gazette* 3.11.1937 p2
19 *Islington Gazette* 24.6.1938 p5
20 *Islington Gazette* 24.6.1938 p5

Chapter Five
1 *Times of India* 12.11.1937 p17
2 *Times of India* 12.11.1937 p17
3 *Times of India* 12.11.1937 p17
4 *Alaway* Football All Around the World p101-2
5 *Times of India* 12.11.1937 p17
6 *Times of India* 12.11.1937 p17
7 *Islington Gazette* 24.6.1938 p5
8 *Alaway* Football All Around the World p103
9 *Alaway* Football All Around the World p103
10 *Star of India* 13.11.1937 p10
11 *Alaway* Football All Around the World p103-4
12 *Times of India* 15.11.1937 p15
13 *Alaway* Football All Around the World p113
14 *Lethbridge Herald* 18.5.1938 p16
15 *San Francisco Chronicle* 4.5.1938 p2H
16 *Times of India* 18.11.1937 p11
17 *Alaway* Football All Around the World p105
18 *Alaway* Football All Around the World p105
19 *Alaway* Football All Around the World p106
20 *Times of India* 19.11.1937 p13
21 *Alaway* Football All Around the World p105
22 *Islington Gazette* 24.6.1938 p5
23 *Islington Gazette* 24.6.1938 p5
24 *Alaway* Football All Around the World p107
25 *Alaway* Football All Around the World p108
26 *Alaway* Football All Around the World p112
27 *Islington Gazette* 8.6.1938 p2
28 *Times of India* 27.11.1937 p12
29 *Islington Gazette* 12.8.1938 p3
30 *Alaway* Football All Around the World p112
31 *San Francisco Chronicle* 4.5.1938 p2H
32 *Alaway* Football All Around the World p108
33 *Islington Gazette* 19.8.1938 p3
34 *Islington Gazette* 19.8.1938 p3
35 *Islington Gazette* 19.8.1938 p3
36 *Islington Gazette* 19.8.1938 p3
37 *Alaway* Football All Around the World p114
38 *Alaway* Football All Around the World p108-110
39 *Alaway* Football All Around the World p110
40 *Islington Gazette* 19.8.1938 p3
41 *Alaway* Football All Around the World p110
42 *Islington Gazette* 19.8.1938 p3
43 *Alaway* Football All Around the World p107
44 *Alaway* Football All Around the World p113
45 *Islington Gazette* 2.9.1938 p4
46 *Alaway* Football All Around the World p113
47 *Islington Gazette* 2.9.1938 p4
48 *Times of India* 31.12.1937 p14
49 *Times of India* 10.1.1938 p12
50 *Malayan Tribune (Singapore)* 3.2.1938 p13
51 *Alaway* Football All Around the World p114
52 *Alaway* Football All Around the World p115

Chapter Six
1 *Malayan Tribune* (Singapore) 3.2.1938 p13
2 *Alaway* Football All Around the World p115
3 *Times of India* 4.1.1938 p13
4 *Alaway* Football All Around the World p115-6
5 *Malayan Tribune* (Singapore) 12.1.1938 p14
6 *Alaway* Football All Around the World p108-110
7 *Islington Gazette* 2.9.1938 p4
8 *Malayan Tribune* (Singapore) 10.1.1938 p14
9 *Malayan Tribune* (Singapore) 12.1.1938 p14
10 *Malaya Tribune* 4.1.1938 p15
11 *Alaway* Football All Around the World p116
12 *Malayan Tribune* (Kuala Lumpar) 17.1.1938 p15

13 *Malayan Tribune* (Kuala Lumpar) 17.1.1938 p15
14 *San Francisco Chronicle* 4.5.1938 p2H
15 *Islington Gazette* 2.9.1938 p4
16 *Malayan Tribune* (Singapore) 24.1.1938 p14
17 *Malayan Tribune* (Singapore) 25.1.1938 p14
18 *Malayan Tribune* (Singapore) 13.1.1938 p15
19 *Malayan Tribune* (Singapore) 31.1.1938 p14
20 *San Francisco Chronicle* 4.5.1938 p2H
21 *Malaya Tribune* 9.2.1938 p11
22 *Malaya Tribune* 9.2.1938 p11
23 *Malaya Tribune* (Singapore) 4.2.1938 p14
24 *Malayan Tribune* (Singapore) 3.2.1938 p13

Chapter Seven
1 *Alaway* Football All Around the World p117
2 *Martin* Miscellanous article from players scrapbook
3 *South China Morning Press* 25.2.1938 p8
4 *Islington Gazette* 28.10.1938 p1
5 *South China Morning Press* 25.2.1938 p8
6 *South China Morning Press* 25.2.1938 p8
7 *South China Morning Press* 26.2.1938 p6
8 *Alaway* Football All Around the World p120-121
9 *South China Morning Post* 2.3.1938 p8
10 *Alaway* Football All Around the World p117-118
11 *Alaway* Football All Around the World p119
12 *San Francisco Chronicle* 4.5.1938 p2H
13 *Wernstedt & Spencer* The Philippine Island World
14 *South China Morning Post* 24.3.1938 p7
15 *South China Morning Post* – 31.3.1938 p6
16 *South China Morning Post* 1.4.1938 p6

Chapter Eight
1 *China Press* 4.4.1938 p4
2 *Alaway* Football All Around the World p121-122
3 *Islington Gazette* 7.10.1938 p3
4 *Alaway* Football All Around the World p122-123
5 *Alaway* Football All Around the World p122-123
6 *Japan Weekly Chronicle* 14.4.1938 p471
7 *Alaway* Football All Around the World p122-123
8 *Alaway* Football All Around the World p123

Chapter Nine
1 *Alaway* Football All Around the World p124
2 *Honolulu Star Bulletin* 16.4.1938 p14
3 *Alaway* Football All Around the World p124
4 *Los Angeles Times* 27.4.1938 p9
5 *San Francisco Chronicle* 1.5.1938 p7H
6 *San Francisco Chronicle* 2.5.1938 p3H
7 *San Francisco Chronicle* 2.5.1938 p3H
8 *San Francisco Chronicle* 5.5.1938 p3H
9 *Winnipeg Free Press* 7.5.1938 p25

Chapter Ten
1 *Lethbridge Herald* 7.5.1938 p16
2 *Alaway* Football All Around the World p125
3 *Winnipeg Free Press* 12.5.1938 p16
4 *Lethbridge Herald* 18.5.1938 p16
5 *Lethbridge Herald* 18.5.1938 p16
6 *Alaway* Football All Around the World p125
7 *Lethbridge Herald* 14.5.1938 p16
8 *Lethbridge Herald* 17.5.1938 p6
9 *Lethbridge Herald* 18.5.1938 p16
10 *Winnipeg Free Press* 21.5.1938 p27
11 *Winnipeg Free Press* 21.5.1938 p27
12 *Winnipeg Free Press* 23.5.1938 p18
13 *Globe & Mail* 26.5.1938 p19
14 *Globe & Mail* 26.5.1938 p19
15 *The Gazette* 28.5.1938 p21
16 *Islington Gazette* 8.6.1938 p2
17 *Winnipeg Free Press* 30.5.1938 p25

Chapter Eleven
1 *Islington Gazette* 2.9.1938 p6
2 *Islington Gazette* 7.10.1938 p3
3 *Islington Gazette* 7.10.1938 p3
4 *Islington Gazette* 7.10.1938 p3
5 *The Times* 1.12.1938 p6
6 *The Gleaner* 9.1.1940 p12

SUBSCRIBERS

Thank you to the following people who made the production of this book possible. Your support is much appreciated.

Tom Blackbourn
Phil Pepperell
Richard Yates
John Mills
Keith Betts
Peter Taylor
Ian Fitzgerald
Barry
Derek Sale
Peter William Brown
John R. Ringrose
Robert S. Bradley
G.G.O. Hyatt
Neville Evans
Mark Hutton
David Hetherington
Dr. Neil F. Morrison
Moyra Woodward
The Phillips Brothers
Tony Slade
Keith Reynolds
Bob Lilliman
Ivan Page
Brian Burt
Amanda Bradley
Morgyn Chipres
Morgyn Chipres
Norman Epps
Barbara Pratt
Norman Shiel
John Cracknell

Gloria Coyne
Ed & Emma Blackbourn
Peter Kolodziej
Andy Sakseide
Rod Fraser
Jane Din
Peter Cavallini
Sherrill Burrows
Michael Cavallini
Vincenzo Regoli
C. Timbrell
Malcolm Wederell
Justin Carcavella
Brian Vandervilt
Rob Pearce
Niall Watt
Tony Mason
Stuart Chatterton
Clare Shelley
Anita Cavallini
Steve Martin
Robert Wooldridge
Chris Parrott
Wagner Jacot Júnior
Mark Walden
Aidan Hamilton
Jan Allwood
Craig Tyreman
Stefan Bokota
Rachel Cripps
Roger Hillman

ALSO BY THIS AUTHOR

Play Up Corinth – A History of the Corinthian F.C. : £17.99 + £3 postage
288 pages, full narrative, 120 illustrations, complete record of games and team line ups

The Wanderers – Five Times F.A. Cup Winners: £9.99 + £1 postage
150 pages, full narrative, complete record of games and team line ups

Available from www.dognduck.net

Or send a cheque payable to Rob Cavallini to
Flat F1, 6 Grove Lane, Kingston, KT1 2SU

Signed copies available on request

COMING SOON

THE CASUALS F.C. 1883-1939
(Expected release date – early 2009)

For further news visit

www.dognduck.net